Faith Under Siege

FAITH UNDER SIEGE

A History Of Unitarian Theology

Anatole Browde, Ph.D.

iUniverse, Inc.
New York   Bloomington

Faith Under Siege
A History of Unitarian Theology

iUniverse books may be ordered through booksellers or by contacting:

iUniverse
1663 Liberty Drive
Bloomington, IN 47403
www.iuniverse.com
1-800-Authors (1-800-288-4677)

ISBN: 978-1-4401-1162-4 (pbk)
ISBN: 978-1-4401-1163-1 (cloth)
ISBN: 978-1-4401-1165-5 (ebk)

LCCN Number: 2008943628

Printed in the United States of America

iUniverse rev. date:6/8/2009

THIS BOOK IS DEDICATED TO
THOSE THAT HAVE INSPIRED ME:

Richard W. Davis
Professor Emeritus
Washington University

UNITARIAN MINISTERS

Earl Holt
Minister of King's Chapel
Boston, Massachusetts

Suzanne Meyers
Minister of the Unitarian Universalist Church
Cheyenne, Wyoming

AND MOST IMPORTANTLY:

My Wife, Jacqueline Rousseau Browde
Who put up with the many hours of research and writing.

Jesus said to Thomas: "Have you believed because you have seen me? Blessed are those who have not seen me yet believe."
New Testament, John 20

Our primary objective is to sustain a humanizing community of concern in which deep, troubling questions may be fearlessly addressed, the mind freed, and the soul nourished. We strive to be a caring community, supportive of the individuals within, involved in the world without.
First Unitarian Church of Saint Louis

Contents

PREFACE

It is perhaps presumptuous to compare a phrase from the Bible with the statement of purpose of a modern Unitarian congregation, but the large gulf between them illustrates the broad spectrum of beliefs in today's Unitarianism. This work started as a journey through Unitarian history to determine whether a theme exists that ties Unitarianism's Christian antecedent to the service formats and sermons used in the modern church. It was a search first for a unique Unitarian theology that not only informed the early churches in Europe and America and second for how this evolved to reconcile conservative Christian Unitarianism with the transcendental movement and Humanism.

Unitarian histories abound, from the works of Earl Morse Wilbur and Conrad Wright to John Buehrens and Forrest Church's *Chosen Faith*. David Bumbrey's *Unitarian Universalist Narrative History* also treats the movement in great detail. Yet the spiritual development of the denomination is not well covered, perhaps because few Unitarian ministers will accept a particular theology, and modern congregations will only tolerate a totally inclusive belief system.

Throughout history Unitarian these ministers have made a journey of faith from other, mostly traditional, Christian denominations. Almost all came to the liberal faith through a rejection of the restrictive concepts of Calvinist predestination, salvation through a profession of the divinity of Christ, and baptism. Some received the call to the ministry while in other occupations and then accepted the challenge of academic preparation, election by a congregation, and the national denomination, student ministry, and internship, a journey that was demanding and sometimes frustrating. Each person thus had to develop his or her faith and theology without doctrinaire guidance. In eighteenth century England, the driving forces were dissatisfaction with the Anglican and Presbyterian churches and a transfusion of Socinian doctrines from Transylvania. It energized two towering figures, Joseph Priestley and Thomas Belsham, who carried the Unitarian message to the dissenters. In the budding United States the seminal events were the acceptance of Unitarianism by Ellery Channing, and the ascension of John Ware to the faculty of Harvard Divinity School. From these modest beginnings, graduates began to crisscross the east and central states, spreading the Unitarian word and founding churches. While early Unitarianism established no prerequisites for the theology of its ministers, there was an underlying theme of an acceptance of either God or a higher power and the preaching of morality based on the Ten Commandments, the Golden Rule, and the Sermon on the Mount. It was faith based, and became the cornerstone of Channing's Unitarian Christianity. Yet the very absence of a mandatory creedal statement of belief or an expression of faith enabled the open discussion of every aspect of religion. This led rapidly to the transcendental movement started by Ralph Waldo Emerson and the concept of absolute religion of Theodore Parker, and churches across the denomination developed systems of faith ranging from Christianity to Secular Humanism.

In 1859, Henry Bellows, the renowned minister of All Soul's Unitarian Church in New York City, discussed the erosion of faith not only in Unitarianism but in all Protestant religion. In an address to the alumni of the Harvard Divinity School, he decried the fact that "knowingness, curiosity, wit, covetousness and publicity…have so largely taken the place of the deeper passions of the soul in which conjugal love, parental care, filial reverence domestic quietude… seem so lamentable in abeyance." He called his address *The Suspense of Faith, A Discourse on the State of the Church*. Totally unheralded in the Unitarian denomination was the 1894 discourse *The Ground of a Living Faith* by Lucelia Learned, wife of the pastor of the Church of the Unity in Saint Louis, discussed in chapter three. The sermon embodies precisely the type of faith now often lacking in modern Unitarian churches, a criticism presaged by Bellows by his remarks about the dilution of a theological foundation for Unitarianism.

Therefore, by the middle of the twentieth century when the Unitarian Universalist Association was founded, it was hard to find a common faith across the denomination. This had the dual effect of intellectualizing the religious aspects of worship and limiting the numbers that would identify themselves as Unitarians. In effect, the concept of faith itself was under siege, to be abandoned at will or to be reinterpreted to include diverse theologies such as pagans, wiccans, Buddhists, and other earth-based beliefs. In many of today's Unitarian churches, any peace to be found in the religious experience of worship is replaced by a discourse on current events, politics, literature, or philosophy. One would hope that a Unitarian theology can be found by comparing Easter sermons since, Easter is the one holiday difficult to discuss without recourse to the role of God and Jesus, but even there no distinct Unitarian theme emerges.

This work presents a search for a comprehensive Unitarian theology through a study of the spiritual development of Unitarianism, starting with its origin in biblical times and continuing with its spread across Europe, England and the United States. It is also an attempt to find a common faith in modern Unitarian churches. Two churches are used as the principal examples for the evolution of a modern belief system: the First Unitarian Church of Cincinnati and the First Unitarian Church of Saint Louis. Both churches are in cities with similar demographics and almost parallel paths of development but with different approaches to religion. This work then concludes with a survey of modern Unitarian faith.

By necessity the main sources of material for this book are Unitarian sermons and the Berry Street essays. Rather than paraphrase them, I have used extensive quotes from both to reflect the theological orientation of their churches and authors. This acts as a compendium of Unitarian thinking about the cornerstone of the religion using the words of its clergy and philosophers. It is, of course, impossible to review the vast reservoir of sermons and writings of all Unitarian ministers. Hopefully those chosen are representative of the breadth not only of our geography but also of our beliefs.

In doing research for this book, I have talked to many ministers and directors of faith development across the denomination. I thank them for their help and support. I am particularly indebted to Walter Herz and Ed Rider, historians of the First Unitarian Church in Cincinnati. They supplied me with a timeline and many of the sermons quoted in chapter three. Melanie Fathman, archivist of First Unitarian Church of Saint Louis, provided access to its stored material and Paul Sprecher, scribe of the Berry Street Conference, who cleared the quoted essays for publication.

In the interest of full disclosure, I have been a Unitarian since 1948, attending churches in Fort Wayne, Baltimore, Washington, D.C., and Seattle. I was active in the First Unitarian Church in Cincinnati from 1955 to 1959 and, since then, in the First Unitarian Church of Saint Louis. It will become obvious that I am a theist with a strong belief in the transcendental identification of the permanent in our Christian origins.

INTRODUCTION

The definition of the term "Unitarian" has vexed ministers and laypeople from the earliest days of the movement to the present. Jack Mendelsohn highlights the problem in his essay *What do you say after you say I am a Unitarian Universalist?* and points out that there is no single answer.[1] If you pride yourself on being a non-creedal church then no definition of the term will satisfy. Some Unitarians consider themselves Christian yet believe Jesus to be man. Others are humanists, bristling at any concept of God and most objecting to salvation, be it universal or individual. Humanists may celebrate Easter and Christmas, but they have trouble with the distinct religious sense of the holidays. The majority of Unitarians fall in the middle, believing in a supernatural power, perhaps a life force or a gentler version of Jehovah, but continuing, as do the others, to object to defining a creed. Thus, with the growth of orthodox Christian beliefs, Unitarianism has been controversial. In one form or another it has been vilified or supported by councils and synods, laypeople and bishops, philosophers and ministers, heretics, humanists, and Christians. In spite of the controversy, the modern Unitarian church arose with a broad spectrum of beliefs, reflecting in the words of its ministers the non-creedal religious liberality of the denomination. Can one then find a path that brings the movement from its early beginnings to a modern unique Unitarian theology? While some continuity exists, Unitarianism is marked primarily by the many divergent streams reflecting the history of the movement and individual acts of a particular church and its members. There is however, within the spectrum of Unitarianism a central belief system, neither as orthodox as the Unitarian Christianity reflected in Boston's King's Chapel, nor as liberal as the Humanism preached in First Church of Minneapolis. Nor is this middle of the road theology consistent with the broad outline of beliefs used by the Unitarian Universalist Association that seeks to eliminate theist references, and indulges in efforts to insure a non-sexist identification of the deity.

When one surveys the sermon topics of Unitarian ministers through two centuries one topic appears with amazing regularity: "What Unitarians Believe." It appears then, that the very fact of having no creed demands the regular and personal affirmation of a system of beliefs that defines a distinct theology. As a prerequisite one must define the word *theology* and how it relates to a non-creedal religion. James Luther Adams, the noted Unitarian scholar and minister, calls it: "faith seeking understanding of yourself and understanding of reality."[2] Note that there is no mention of God or a higher power; instead, it is an expression of the human quality that acknowledges that there are no ready answers to the central questions of beginning of life or death. Unitarians must therefore strive for the morality and ethics that makes life better on earth. Perhaps a more enduring faith is eloquently described by Paul Tillich when he talks about *Spirit* and *Spiritual Presence*:

> The Spirit can work in you, awakening the desire to strive towards the sublime against the profanity of the average day. The Spirit can give you the courage to say "yes" to life in spite of the destructiveness you have experienced around you and within you... The Spirit can make you love, with the divine love, someone you profoundly dislike or in whom you have no interest...These are works of the Spirit, signs of the Spiritual Presence with us and in us. In view of these manifestations, who can assert that he is without Spirit? Who can say that he is in no way the bearer of Spirit?[3]

This could be a description of the higher power, or life force, or even God, that "middle of the road" Unitarian churches profess, but it is also an open invitation to accept any and all systems of belief. It is at the heart of a paradox: no single answer exists to Mendelsohn's question, thus faith becomes the enemy of intellect. The very freedom to believe anything can persuade a Unitarian to abandon religion. Conversely, those that feel an emotional need for spiritual fulfillment may return to the more traditional environment of Christianity or Judaism.

It was not always so. The modern Unitarian church is an outgrowth of a search for a rational faith that spans the period from the early days of Christianity, through its English roots, to the transformation of the movement to a modern religion as practiced in America. More than any other religious denomination, Unitarianism has evolved dramatically from the Arian heresy of the third century to the Humanism of today. Thus, any history of the movement or of individual congregations must examine as a baseline a spectrum of beliefs against which church theology can be measured. This task is made difficult because even within one congregation there is often no unity of belief, no creed, and no service format. Members are free to accept the Bible with its miracles, as Ellery Channing did in Boston during the early nineteenth century, or reject any mention of God, as John Dietrich did in his ministry in Minneapolis from 1916 to 1938. Furthermore every Unitarian church evolved theologically as ministers came and went. Often, what started as a congregation of Unitarian Christians, ended theist or humanist. Neville Buch was also concerned about the denominational drift to an all-inclusive acceptance of beliefs. In his article published in the Meadville-Lombard Journal of Liberal Religion, *Preliminary Conclusions in the Search of Philosophical Grounds for Contemporary Unitarian Identity,* he first describes nineteenth century English Unitarian James Martineau's view that a distinct Unitarian identity was unnecessary, and then made these observations:

> As helpful as his philosophical theology was to articulate Unitarian belief, his advocacy of a diluted Unitarian identity in a free and loose association across the theological spectrum did the Unitarian movement a great disservice. He fails to foresee that such a free and loose association ended up with many

liberal religionists maintaining Unitarian beliefs within their own liberal Protestant identity, and casting the Unitarian shell aside, robbed Unitarian identity of any mainstream credibility it was due... and hence today Unitarians have become largely irrelevant in the main theological discourse.

Buch then postulated that in Universalism all human entities are valued equally. He continued: "What, however has crept into Unitarian Universalism is a non-philosophically defined interpretation which says...all *beliefs* are valued equally, such as no belief can be condemned as false, wrong, mistaken, etc."[4] This leads to the conclusion that a Unitarian chooses through logic and not through emotion. Faith does not enter into the selection; it has been devalued. In my opinion this caused the denomination to become too dry and emotionally barren and has inhibited the growth one finds in other denominations.

To understand modern Unitarianism one must first define the original branches that gave birth to the movement. Several paths to Unitarianism arose in the early days of the church: Arianism, Socinianism, Arminianism, Transcendentalism and Deism. As the name of the denomination implies, Unitarians through the ages rejected the conservative Christian view of God in three persons, Father, Son and Holy Ghost, insisting instead on a single unified God. Some argue that Unitarian concepts reflect the three early synoptic gospels. These were written before the Trinity was accepted around 50 A.D., when Paul was preaching the divinity of Christ in Asia Minor. The first challenge to the Christian view of God in three persons came from Arius, a bishop of the church in the fourth century. He asserted that Christ was made in time by God, was of God, but because of his subsequent creation by God, could not be equal to God. Under Bishop Athanasius, the Council of Nicea in 325 rejected this interpretation. Instead the Council incorporated the classic Trinitarian expression of faith in the creedal statement that bears his name and is still used today by most traditional Christian denominations. Through the ages, however, a sizable number of the Christian clergy continued to support Arianism, even though rulers in Catholic and Protestant Europe deemed it heretical and often punished it by execution. Socinianism, in turn, arose in the sixteenth century as an outgrowth of the Arian faith and reflected the belief of Lelio and Faustus Sozzini that Jesus was human but divinely inspired. Both the Catholic and Calvinist churches deemed this to be a direct assault on orthodoxy. The most famous advocate of Socinian views at the time, Michael Servetus, debated the doctrine with Calvin in Geneva in 1553 and was ordered to recant. When he refused he was burnt at the stake. In 1559 Faustus Sozzini was denounced by the inquisition and forced to flee from his hometown of Siena, first to Switzerland and then to Poland.[5]

Despite fierce European persecution of both Arians and Socinians Unitarianism did not quietly disappear. In the Middle Ages, because the area that became Hungary was quite isolated from the imposition of orthodox Catholicism, the province of Transylvania contained many churches with Arian leaning clergy. When the reformation swept across parts of Europe, Transylvania was ready to accept Calvinist beliefs, but, in order to avoid religious strife during the 1550s, its ruler, John Sigismund, adopted an edict of religious tolerance and Unitarianism began to flourish.

In his book *The Epic of Unitarianism* David Parke described this transformation:

> Nominally Catholic until the sixteenth century, Transylvania was converted to Protestantism between 1520, when the first Lutheran books and missionaries arrived, and 1566 when the government disestablished the Catholic Church. In 1561 John Sigismund became King of Transylvania, the first and only Unitarian king in history... Above all, he was deeply interested in religion, and sought to pacify the conflicts between Roman Catholics, Greek Orthodox, Lutherans, Calvinists, and Unitarians in his realm. His closest adviser was Dr. Giorgio Biandrata who had helped establish AntiTrinitarianism in Poland. Out of personal conviction, therefore, and practical political considerations, he fostered a policy of open discussion and broad toleration of all viewpoints which made Transylvania the freest country in

Europe in religious matters. Transylvania's first decree of religious toleration came in 1557. It was renewed in 1563. Five years later, after the Diet had unanimously made a request that John "declare and strengthen" the prior decrees, the young King issued this famous Act of Religious Tolerance and Freedom of Conscience:

His Majesty, our Lord, in what manner he – together with his realm [i.e., the Diet]– legislated in the matter of religion at the previous Diets, in the same manner now, in this Diet, he reaffirms that in every place the preachers shall preach and explain the Gospel each according to his understanding of it, and if the congregation like it, well, if not, no one shall compel them for their souls would not be satisfied, but they shall be permitted to keep a preacher whose teaching they approve.[6]

With freedom of religion now officially recognized in Transylvania, the Socinians established there the first church to openly preach Unitarian beliefs. In 1566, Francis David had become superintendent of the Protestant churches. He had been educated in Wittenberg, where he became thoroughly versed in both Lutheran theology and Calvinism. By 1568 he had become convinced that the doctrine of God in three persons was false and accepted Socinian views.[7] Freedom of worship was severely curtailed, however, when Istvan Batori came to the throne after John Sigismund died in 1572, and the country reverted to a rigid Calvinist state religion. In 1579, Francis David was arrested, sentenced to life imprisonment, and died shortly thereafter. In spite of this, his main contribution to Unitarianism, the Hungarian Unitarian Catechism, survived and is used by some European churches to this day. The document was brought to Poland by Faustus Socinus, and in 1609 it was rewritten and published as the Racovian Catechism.

Arminianism was patterned after Jacobus Arminius, a Dutch theologian of the sixteenth century who rejected the Calvinist theory of selection by infinite grace. Arminians asserted that a loving God could not damn all mankind because of Adam's fall. This was an outgrowth of Origen's original theory, formulated at the beginning of the third century, that all God's creatures, even Satan, were capable of salvation. The designation of a few for salvation by the grace and death and resurrection of Jesus was inconsistent with the concept of a loving and all-knowing God. Arminianism became incorporated in Methodism but strenuously rejected by the Puritans, was embraced by American clerics of the seventeenth and eighteenth century who would soon become Christian Unitarians or Universalists. Indeed, during the 1770s, a Massachusetts Baptist minister, Elihanan Winchester, began to doubt the orthodox Calvinist principles of election and predestination and refused to call on sinners to repent. He was expelled from the Baptist denomination and moved south to preach a doctrine of universal salvation. Whereas the Harvard-bred Unitarians were an elite group of the wealthy, Winchester addressed the poor and downtrodden, even those that were slaves. In 1779, he travelled north to Philadelphia and accepted a call to a Baptist church. He was careful to remain a Baptist, at least nominally, but by 1782 the Philadelphia church was unofficially identified as Universalist. Winchester preached the principles of universal salvation that God is love, and purposefully designed the world to make his people happy. In his view, Christ did not die in vain but rather to destroy all sin, and would save all mankind. In 1803, the Universalists adopted their profession of faith which proclaims "the belief that the Holy Scriptures of the Old and New Testaments contain a revelation of the character of God, and of the duty, interest, and final destination of mankind; that there is one God whose nature is Love, revealed in Lord Jesus Christ, by one Holy Spirit of Grace, who will finally restore the whole family of mankind to holiness and happiness, and that holiness and true happiness are inseparably connected, and that believers ought to be careful to maintain order, and practice good works; for these things are good and profitable to men."[8] It was left it to the individual churches and societies to adopt articles of faith best suited to their circumstances.

It was the start of the Universalist denomination. In 1811, Hosea Ballou published *A Treatise on Atonement*, a book that would become famous in liberal religion. He argued both by example and cogent logic that an infinite God would not impart infinite guilt on man. He further demonstrated that it defies reason that a loving God would establish sin in the world through Adam and then pass this sin throughout mankind. Finally, it would be illogical that God would create someone in human form, guiltless, only to destroy him in order to atone for the sins of all mankind. As an example he cited:

> Suppose we [postulate a] father and his ten children: suppose the father has provisions enough for the whole, and his object in the bestowing of it upon them is to cause the greatest possible happiness among his children. Which way would good sense and parental affection choose, either to feed five to the full, and starve the rest to death, that their dying groans might give the others a better appetite and their food a good relish, or to let them all be hungry enough to relish their food well, and all alike partake of it? I would further argue that, as man is constituted to enjoy happiness, on moral principles (to the knowledge of which principles we come by degrees), it is as reasonable to believe that all men were intended to obtain a consummate knowledge of the moral principles of their nature as that any of Adam's race were. There is not an individual of the whole family of man who is perfectly satisfied with those enjoyments which earth and time afford him; the soul is constituted for nobler pleasures, which to me is an evidence that God has provided for all men some better things than can be found in earthly enjoyments, where we find but little except vanity and disappointment. There is an immortal desire in every soul for future existence and happiness.[9]

This concept was easier to understand and more attractive to non-elites than Unitarian theology and even established preachers began to weave it into their sermons. Although many did not immediately shift to a liberal religion, their sermons demonstrated that they were open to the message. Indeed, the concept that Jesus

Christ was filled with the spirit of love, and that his life revealed his depth of faith and manifested the great and amazing love of God, might well describe the early beliefs of Unitarian Christianity. It was a declaration that demonstrated how to incarnate divine love in individual lives and reveal it by words and deeds.

Transcendentalism rejected the miracles of revealed religion and asserted that humans intuitively grasp the wonders of the world. It believed in the essential unity of creation, the goodness of humanity, and the supremacy of insight over logic and reason. First annunciated by Ralph Waldo Emerson, it was never clearly defined, but it would lead to Humanism and deism and, in its most extreme form, reject all aspects of supernatural religion. David Bebbington likened it to the British holiness movements, and called it *sentimentalized moralism* and the core of American Romanticism, an appellation that Emerson would surely have rejected. [10] As the First World War unfolded in Europe and America became increasingly involved, Humanism in a very pure form was adopted by a number of Unitarians, who harkened back to the Greek philosophy of Socrates and found confirmation in works by David Hume and Edmund Burke. They expressed skepticism towards miracles in religion, doubted the presence of a supreme being, and rejected any claim of immortality. The opposite of Humanism, within the spectrum of Unitarian thought, was deism (or, as it is often called, theism), a belief in a higher power and a feeling that random processes cannot explain what we are, see, and feel on this earth, thus evoking a strong conviction that there is a supreme being. Martineau, an English Unitarian nineteenth century minister and friend of many liberal ministers of his time, perhaps expressed these beliefs best when he created a very non- doctrinaire, deist point of view. In his essay on the Christian Student he asked:

> What indeed is true theology? It is the knowledge of God. By its very definition therefore it must be co-extensive with the fields of his manifestations, and we have something to learn and report wherever his trace has been left…He is Agent and Disposer in outward Nature. He communes with the inmost individual soul. He is the Providence of Collective Humanity…[11]

Martineau maintained that the first task of someone searching for a faith was to find the religious interpretation of the physical sciences, to conceive the meaning of natural laws, and to relate how they interface with God's causality. The second task was to determine the relation of the individual soul to a divine power and to explain how the free human personality is thrown into "the sweeping tides of pantheistic power." Thus Martineau insisted that ministers of any faith must be able to know what they mean when they speak of will, conscience, and reason. The third and final task was to unravel what was meant by divine revelation, specifically questioning the Protestant interpretation of religion as an all-pervasive influence in human affairs.

With such widely divergent views, it was somewhat of a miracle that both in England and in America Unitarianism flourished. In each country Unitarian central organizations were formed, not so much to dictate religious thought but rather to further the movement, educate its clergy, and coordinate the appointment of ministers. Equally importantly, the denominations in both countries started to establish publications that would reflect the diverse interpretations of Unitarianism. Only in the late twentieth century did Unitarianism depart from its root values in Christianity, embracing such a wide range of beliefs that some doubt the very concept of it being a religious denomination. Thus the principles of the present day Unitarian Universalist Association (UUA) include this statement:

> The living tradition which we share draws from many sources:
>
> Direct experience of that transcending mystery and wonder affirmed in all cultures, which moves us to a renewal of the spirit and an openness to the forces which create and uphold life;
>
> Words and deeds of prophetic women and men, which challenge us to confront powers and structures of evil with justice, compassion and the transforming power of love;

Wisdom from the world's religions, which inspires us in our ethical and spiritual life;

Jewish and Christian teachings, which call us to respond to God's love by loving our neighbors as ourselves;

Humanist teachings, which counsel us to heed the guidance of reason and the results of science, and warn us against idolatries of the mind and spirit;

Spiritual teachings of Earth-centered traditions, which celebrate the sacred circle of life and instruct us to live in harmony with the rhythms of nature.

The very breadth of allowable beliefs and absence of dogmatic pronouncements in Unitarianism enabled any United States church to have a theological orientation based on its social environment rather than on UUA beliefs or the views of the congregation and its minister. These beliefs often became a snapshot of liberal political thinking of the present without reference to its antecedents. In 2000, as a reaction to this trend, the American Unitarian Conference (AUC) was born, "dedicated to the renewal of the historic Unitarian faith." Its statement of beliefs is very different from that of the UUA:

Our Religious Principles:

God's presence is made known in a myriad of ways. Religion should promote a free and responsible search for truth, meaning, communion and love.

Reason is a gift from God. Religion should embrace reason and its progeny, including the scientific enterprise which explores God's creation.

Free will is a gift from God. Religion should assist in the effort to find a path that exercises that gift in a responsible, constructive and ethical manner.

Conscious of the complexity of creation, of the limits of human understanding and of humanity's capacity for evil in the name of religion, we hold that humility, religious tolerance and freedom of conscience should be a central part of any religious experience.

Religious experience is most fulfilling in the context of a tradition. Our religious tradition is the Unitarian tradition, which emphasizes the importance of reason in religion, tolerance and the unity of God.

Revelation is ongoing. Religion should draw inspiration not only from its own tradition but from other religious traditions, philosophy and the arts. Although paying due regard for the hard lessons learned in the past and to the importance of religious tradition, religion should not be stagnant but should employ reason and religious experience to evolve in a constructive, enlightened and fulfilling way.

Conscious of the spiritual and material needs of our fellow men and women, the evil they may be subjected to and the tragedies they may endure, works of mercy and compassion should be a part of any religious experience.

Few modern Unitarian churches or ministers have adopted the AUC principles, since they would represent an imposition of theism on a denomination that prides itself on total freedom of belief. The British Unitarian movement's statement of beliefs perhaps represents a middle ground, since it recognizes the need for religion but not necessarily a definition of God:

We believe that:

Everyone has the right to seek truth and meaning for themselves.

The fundamental tools for doing this are your own life experience, your reflection upon it, your intuitive understanding and the promptings of your own conscience.

The best setting for this is a community that welcomes you for who you are, complete with your beliefs, doubts and questions.

We can be called religious 'liberals:

religious because we unite to celebrate and affirm values that embrace and reflect a greater reality than self.

liberal because we claim no exclusive revelation or status for ourselves; because we afford respect and toleration to those who follow different paths of faith.

We are called 'Unitarians':

because of our traditional insistence on divine unity, the oneness of God.

because we affirm the essential unity of humankind and of creation

The following chapters will describe the English movement and Unitarian development in America. The history of two modern mid-American Unitarian churches, the First Unitarian Church of Cincinnati and the First Unitarian Church of Saint Louis, will be used to highlight the evolution of theist Unitarian theology. Lastly, the belief systems existing in today's Unitarian churches will be examined through sermons and writings of its ministers, to arrive at a more joyful Unitarianism that reestablishes faith as a guiding principle for modern congregations.

CHAPTER 1:

*From Heresy To Dissent British
Unitarianism In The 18th And 19th Century*

Unitarian beliefs came to England in the seventeenth century and the movement matured during the eighteenth and nineteenth centuries. While small in number, British Unitarians built English industry, fought in Parliament for freedoms we now take for granted, created a heritage of freedom of religion, and spawned the social action of English Unitarian men and women who brought about social improvement and universal suffrage. Many Americans are familiar with the early Unitarianism of our founding fathers; fewer know how it began in England. From Jefferson through the Adams presidencies, many of the leading figures in American political life were Unitarian. They were able to practice their religion because the young country was founded on the rock of separation of church and state. This was not the case in Britain, which had experienced violent encounters between Anglicans, Catholics and dissenters.

In England, Henry VIII, who ruled from 1509 to 1547, founded the Church of England during the 1530s, and, by 1534, decreed it to be the state religion. An official Book of Prayer was published in 1552, and eleven years later a creed was developed, the famous Thirty-Nine Articles, totally Trinitarian in nature. Those who would not or could not accept these were named Dissenters, and they, and Catholics, were severely persecuted as the Tudors adopted a Protestant religion that became the Church of England. The 1662 Act of Uniformity divided these denominations into an established Anglican Church and classified dissenters as non-conformists.

By the time George I took office in 1714, dissent in England was widespread and powerful. Yet English and American religious history can be understood only by covering the development of dissent from its Anglican roots, specifically by studying the Presbyterian movement that began in the late sixteenth century. As Jeremy Goring points out, this occurred along two very different paths, one in Scotland, and another, very different, in the more liberal English churches.[12]

The logical starting point for tracing the growth of English Unitarianism thus must be 1563, when the Anglican Church issued its creedal statements and became, de facto, the official religion of England, and remained so, except for the short period when Catholicism was preferred by the ruler. After the 1688 Glorious Revolution, the Anglican Church was supreme. Within it, however, there were a number of parishes and ministers who objected to the method of governing the church— the Episcopacy, effectively a hierarchical scheme, with little, if any, autonomy by individual churches. Bolam called those favoring greater self-government *Church Puritans* or *Parish Puritans*.[13] They would soon call themselves Presbyterians, the term signifying parish control of ministers and liturgy, the presbyters being a local board of governance but with no power to administer the sacraments. The term at first had little theological significance, though there were distinct differences between the view of the Scottish Presbyterian Church and that of the newly named English Presbyterian Church. The former was strongly Calvinistic, the latter much less dogmatic. In fact, it is difficult to distinguish between true English Presbyterians and those who became independent dissenters. Yet the very fact that there was local autonomy enabled some Presbyterian ministers to drift towards Arminianism. Their composition, societal position, and political affiliation reflected the views of those English churchmen who objected to the hierarchical makeup of the Anglican Church, and many of these ministers were removed from their Anglican parishes. This *Ejection*, as it would be called, climaxed in 1661, when Presbyterian ministers who desired modification of the Anglican Prayer Book, and took the liberty of departing from its text in their service, were evicted from their parishes. In addition the compromise agreement between the Scottish Presbyterians and their English brethren, the so-called Worcester Covenant of 1642, was cast aside, and by the end of the year, the Corporation Act was passed, requiring that all office holders had to accept the full rites of the Church of England as described in the Thirty-Nine Articles. This was followed in 1665 by the Five Mile Act, further restricting the activities of the dissenting Presbyterians, and by the Test Act of 1673, which required all members of the government to swear allegiance to the Crown and to receive the sacraments of the Church of England at least once a year.

The Presbyterian Church, whether it liked it or not, had become a member of Dissent and was now excluded from the Church of England. While Presbyterians might try hard to be accepted as part of the established church, they never again would be able to claim any distinction from other dissenting denominations. Until the 1689 Toleration Act was enacted, the movement remained illegal, even though Presbyterians had objected only to church governance and not to imposed beliefs. Yet even that act did not grant freedom of worship, allowing instead the Presbyterian church organization to exist outside of the Episcopal hierarchy of the Church of England. Dogma was still strictly Trinitarian and required acceptance of all parts of the Thirty-Nine Articles other than those dealing with church administration. Nine years later, the Blasphemy Act made very clear that only the literal interpretation of the Trinity would be accepted. Theology thus became a matter of dispute, as did the classification of Presbyterianism as part of dissent. Some accepted their status as dissenters and left the movement to become the Independents, later the Congregationalists. The irony of this nomenclature is that initially, the Independents were conservative Christians who could relate more to Calvinist precepts than the Presbyterians did. One must stress, however, that as the seventeenth century began, neither the Presbyterians nor the Independents considered themselves separated from the Anglican Church. Only with the Corporation and Test Acts would their isolation become complete. The full spectrum of religious beliefs therefore included Anglicans, mostly in good standing with the government, Catholics who were persecuted and barred from office, and a growing number of sects called Dissenters, among them the Presbyterians, the Independents, and a growing tide of Methodists, Baptists and Quakers. Yet the liberal dissenting movement would not capture the imagination of the general populace; in 1773 only some seven hundred congregations in England and ninety congregations in Wales professed to be Presbyterian, Unitarian or Independent.[14]

Most dangerous, however for Anglican clerics and rulers were those that foreswore the Trinity. Their beliefs were punished by burning. It was not unusual for someone like Thomas Beverley, an Anglican minister, in 1694 to submit a paper to Parliament in which he damned apostasy and condemned the heresies that, according to him, showed that Christ's coming was near. He concluded that:

> … since the Reformation, Socinian and Arrian Unitarianism have Vyed one another to shew the Apostasy's Times not expired. At the end of those Times, All Spirits Denying the Son of God shall be Damned to Everlasting Darkness, from which they Rose; and the Kingdom of the Great Son of Man, God over All, Blessed for Ever, shall enter its Succession, Even so Lord Jesus Come Quickly.

In Britain of the sixteenth and seventeenth centuries, Unitarians were universally damned. Beverley clearly felt that their continued presence showed that the Antichrist was not yet tamed. Were they to be converted quickly it might be a sign that the time of Christ's coming was near. In the context of British religious life and political environment, Beverly's statement came only six years after 1688. The memory of Mary Tudor, who assiduously persecuted and executed non-Catholics, was still fresh, and all movements dissenting from the state-established Anglican Church, as well as non-Trinitarians and Catholics, were forbidden to practice their religion. In contrast, under Elizabeth I religious dissent arose by clerics who rejected the concepts of predestination, and began to gravitate to the concept of a loving God who would not condemn mankind to everlasting suffering.

During the seventeenth century, several English clergymen became exposed to Socinian doctrines through travels in Europe. A number of anti-Trinitarians, usually described as Arians, suffered burning. In Ireland, as early as 1326, Adam Duff was executed for his belief in a single, non-triune- god. In England anti-Trinitarians were executed starting in 1551. George van Parris, a Flemish surgeon was the first, with six more laymen following him to the stake in the next seventy years. In March 1612, Bartholomew Legate was burned at Smithfield, and a month later Edward Wightman suffered the same fate at Litchfield. Both were considered to be Arians. As late as 1697, a youth named Pakenham was hanged at Edinburgh on the charge of heretical blasphemy. Although these were the only executions of this kind, it was clear that the English government felt duty bound to stamp out this belief. According to Tarrant, a letter sent by Archbishop Neile of York to Bishop Laud in 1639, refers to Wightman's case, stating that another man, Trendall, deserved the same sentence. A few years later, Paul Best, a scholarly gentleman who had travelled in Poland and Transylvania and adopted anti-Trinitarian views was sentenced by vote of the House of Commons to be hanged for denying the Trinity. The ordinance drawn up in 1648 by the Puritan authorities was incredibly vindictive against those they judged to be heretical. Happily, Oliver Cromwell and his Independents were conscious of considerable variety of opinion in their own ranks, and Cromwell secured Best's liberation. [15]

In 1650 John Biddle, a graduate of Oxford and teacher at Gloucester, began to question the accepted doctrine of the Trinity and held Socinian meetings in London. He also fell victim to Oliver Cromwell. Biddle was imprisoned several times between 1644 and 1662. In 1655, more than ten years after Biddle's first imprisonment, he was sent to the Scilly Islands and was allowed a yearly allowance for maintenance, obviously to spare him a worse fate. A few months before Cromwell's death, he was brought back to London and released. When he continued to preach anti-Trinitarianism he was arrested again in 1662 and shortly thereafter died in prison.[16]

The first Protestant theologian to preach Arianism in England was Samuel Clarke (1675–1729). An Anglican preacher for Queen Anne, he maintained that Christ was created by God, and while divine, had a lesser stature than God. In 1664, the Racovian Catechism, the Socinian profession of faith, was translated and reprinted in English. It detailed the required knowledge of God and Jesus Christ and annunciated the Unitarian response that "by nature he is a true man."[17] By the start of the eighteenth century, one finds a number of Presbyterian ministers preaching Arianism and Socinianism so much so that in 1714 John Cumming, an orthodox Presbyterian minister, felt it necessary to condemn the doctrines from the pulpit. He characterized the adherents of such heterodoxy as "bound to believe nothing of which they have not a distinct idea. Socinianism and Arianism threaten to lay the axe to the root of Christianity."[18] Even earlier, in 1700, Anglican preachers and laymen had launched an attack on Unitarians. One of these, Nathaniel Taylor, wrote:

> For once men have taken one step over the Fatal Precipice…down they tumble apace with greater speed, till they drop into the Lake of Open Infidelity; and whither their Next fall will be is easy to determine,…We have Proof of this in some of the Foreign Unitarians. They began with denying the Deity and Satisfaction of Christ. Thence Franscicus Davidis, Glirius and Others proceeded to deny the Lawfulness of giving Religious Worship to Him; with whom in This, our English Unitarians who are their Spawn, do generally fall in.[19]

Robert Webb maintains that the view of Jesus as a lesser divinity than God became widespread among those Anglicans, "who were rationally oriented and scripturally defined," but even more in the Presbyterian denomination.[20] Indeed, in the eighteenth century, it was this sect with its open expression of Socinian views that would evolve into English Unitarianism. At the same time, there arose two extremely orthodox Christian movements, the Evangelicals and a form of the Anglican faith that adopted Calvin's views. The Evangelicals believed in salvation through good works, while the Calvinists adhered to the old form of predestination. The movements were directed specifically at conversion of the poor, offering a better life in the hereafter to counter a populace impoverished and wearied by the Napoleonic wars. While Protestant dissent reached its peak in the mid- 1800s, Unitarianism also grew, and its members began an association with liberal Anglicans that became a major factor in English political, social, and intellectual life. In the middle of the century, some dissenters rejected outright the Trinitarian concepts annunciated in the Nicean Creed. Within the Unitarian denomination ministers James Pierce, Theophilus Lindsey and Joseph Priestley advocated a modified Socianian view. It attracted a segment of the population wealthier than the average, better educated, and socially prominent, and it consisted of Christians who rejected the threat of eternal damnation. They never were a large group, but they were influential way beyond their number.

Early in the eighteenth century, the Presbyterian denomination was moving towards a split, specifically over the question of whether Jesus was divine. In the famous Salter's Hall meetings during February 1719, Presbyterian ministers debated this question. Although the orthodox view of Jesus won, it was by only four votes. As a result, in subsequent years many Presbyterian churches turned to Unitarianism, while others declared for the Independents.[21] Gordon Bolam attributes to Presbyterians a long-standing independence in interpreting the Bible. Even though they asserted that they were strictly adhering to it, their higher social standing and education led to the more enlightened view that theories of predestination, original sin, and the Trinity, were non-scriptural. It must be underscored, however, that, in the eighteenth and nineteenth century, most Unitarian ministers and their congregations believed they were Christians, accepted the Bible as divinely inspired, and, above all, accepted an all-powerful deity. They encouraged individual interpretation of the Bible, were non-creedal, and rejected the sacrificial view of atonement and eternal punishment.[22] In effect they started as Arminians and rapidly became Christian Unitarians. During the same period the General Baptists also went through a crisis of belief and turned Arminian. Those that rejected the concept of eternal punishment were excommunicated, based on Christ's words in Matthew Chapter 25: "Depart from me you cursed, into the eternal fire prepared for the devil". This orthodox Protestant view of eternal damnation was rejected by many Baptists, causing them to turn to Universalism. Their argument was that an all-merciful God would not condemn even a hardened sinner to such drastic and everlasting punishment. There would be a limit to suffering and thereafter the soul would be at peace.

The central belief of Unitarians was built around a single, all-loving God. Jesus Christ might be divinely inspired, but he was human. As David Young, an English Unitarian, described him, Jesus was endowed "with the passions and emotions of man, commissioned to preach religious truth and himself the achiever of perfection."[23] Unitarians rejected a universal creed, feeling that each person could establish his own system of belief. The unity of God was ascribed to the early gospels since they did not mention the Trinity. This led each minister to preach his own theology. Joseph Priestley believed in man's bodily ascension to heaven, while others, freely admitting that they did not know how resurrection might have occurred, were convinced that God would accept all mankind. There was no punishment for original sin. The sacraments also had different meanings from those that orthodox Protestants had adopted and adapted from the Catholic Church. Baptism was a dedication of parents to the education of their child to Christianity and the service of God; it was not a prerequisite for salvation. Communion was not a universal practice and was believed to be a commemoration, rather than a reenactment of Christ's agony. The dilemma of biblical miracles troubled many early Unitarian ministers. Robert Webb attributes their views to David Hume and David Hartley. Priestley espoused another mixture of miraculous beliefs, accepting as a miracle the rapid spread of Christianity throughout the western world but rejecting other miracle stories that did not have convincing acceptance among the early Christians. He required an explicit statement of some degree of human witness.[24]

The expansion of the British Unitarian movement started in 1760 when Theophilus Lindsey turned to Unitarianism, Lindsey, originally an Anglican minister, had been the Vicar of Catterick and came to Unitarianism without passing through the preliminary stage of Arianism.[25] He abandoned his living to come to London, rented rooms in Essex Street, and used them for religious services based on Unitarian principles. Lindsey's message was echoed in Leeds and

Birmingham by the preaching of Priestley, whom Robert Webb calls the source of a major English school of thought and action.[26] At that time non-Trinitarian dissent was still proscribed, even after the Toleration Act of 1689 was passed, as it did not absolve those who denied the Trinity. Nor were they immunized by the Blasphemy Act of 1698, which prescribed heavy penalties for the denial. Neither act was vigorously enforced, though Richard Carlisle and others were prosecuted under the Blasphemy Act in 1819, even though the Unitarian Toleration Act was passed by Parliament in 1813. Indeed the Test and Corporation acts, which prevented all dissenters from holding office unless they partook of the Anglican Church communion, were still in force and would be until 1828.

Priestley, known in science for his discovery of oxygen, had adopted the Arian faith while attending Daventry Academy in 1750. By 1769, he had become convinced of the totally human nature of Jesus without however abandoning a belief in an all-seeing and powerful God, and he joined Lindsey at the Essex Street Chapel. He had become converted to this view by his study of works by Hartley who developed a theory called *Necessarianism*. Hartley asserted that actions of individuals, having no ability to overcome the relation between cause and effect once motives remained constant, would always achieve the same result. He denied special providence and divine intercession in the lives of men and also rejected the theory of Christ's atonement for all mankind.[27] The Necessarian belief was also taken up by Thomas Belsham, a Unitarian minister and author. His *Elements of the Philosophy of the Mind, and of Moral Philosophy* was described in the Edinburgh Review. According to the unnamed reviewer, Belsham preached "materialism, necessity and the selfish obligation to virtue."[28] He questioned the concept of the survival of the soul after death, his view being called by the reviewer *annihilation*, and believed that it was necessary to resist temptation, thus creating a greater good on earth. The review is mute on the subject of Christ, but it is known that Belsham shared the belief of Priestley. In 1782, Priestley had moved to Birmingham and there published his *History of the Corruptions of Christianity*, which asserted that the beliefs of the primitive church had been Unitarian and that all later modifications were corruptions. He traveled extensively in the budding United States, but, as described in chapter two, his theology would be rejected by some American Unitarians.

Priestley and the Unitarians supported the French and American revolutions and thus antagonized both the Whigs, led by Edmund Burke, and the Tories in Parliament. In the last decade of the eighteenth century, several attempts had again been made to repeal the Test and Corporation Acts, with Henry Beaufoy speaking eloquently for repeal in 1787 and 1789, and Charles Fox continuing the fight in 1790.[29] Even though all of dissent was working for repeal, when the bill came up for a third vote in 1790, it was rejected by a large majority. The rejection can be traced to a drastic change in the British political climate. Most Unitarians were Foxite Whigs, and their campaign to repeal the Test and Corporation Acts had frightened many Anglican Tory conservatives, who were appalled by Unitarian support of the French Revolution. Anglican ministers launched bitter attacks against them. Priestley in particular roused conservative wrath, and was accused of being an enemy of state and church. In 1791, this agitation caused the Birmingham riots and a mob burned Unitarian and Dissenting chapels and houses of church members, including Priestley's house and laboratory. Soon-to-be Tories denied that the riots were religiously motivated. They ascribed the riots to revulsion of people against the Unitarian celebration of the French revolution, and dubbed the protest purely political. In May of 1792, Samuel Whitbread, incensed at what he contended was an attack on dissent, called for a parliamentary inquiry. He maintained that Anglican clergymen had preached against Unitarians in the days before the riot, that rioters had used the slogan of *God and King* as they destroyed Unitarian property, and that the Birmingham authorities had acquitted most of the rioters. His motion for an inquiry was defeated.[30] The London Times reported the Birmingham riots with much indignation, but blamed the Unitarians:

> Enjoying the blessings of freedom and protected in their Civil and Religious rights by a Constitution which has raised their country to a high eminence of Commercial Wealth and National Glory, it was natural for sensible Englishmen to revolt at the idea

of poisoning the minds of the lower class with those
wild and frantic notions of the demolition of Crowns
and establishment of the RIGHTS OF MAN, which
have destroyed the real liberty of France...[31]

Priestley did not help the Unitarian cause by his involvement with
the French government. In September 1792 he was excoriated by
Tories after the press revealed that he was offered French citizenship
and was invited to become a delegate to their National Convention.
He accepted the citizenship but declined to be a delegate on the
grounds that he was committed to "philosophy and theology."[32]
During 1792 Priestley moved to London, and three years later he
decided to emigrate to the United States. Several Unitarian ministers
were deeply influenced by Priestley, among them Michael Maurice,
whose son Frederick Dennison Maurice would become an Anglican
minister and would practice a much more liberal faith, very close to
Universalism.

In the early part of the nineteenth century the evangelical
movement was at its peak, but at the same time the dissenting
denominations were far from united in their beliefs. The focus of
dissenting evangelicals was a Christ centered faith, with the goal of
achieving conversion that established the human connection with
atonement. At the same time the General Baptist Assembly was
moving the other way, closer to a Unitarian position. By mid-century
some of the more traditional denominations, among them the
Anglican Church, had slowly accepted incarnation and other beliefs
very close to Arminianism. It thus became natural that Unitarians
and Anglicans would associate, especially when they shared cultural
values and common objectives of philanthropic action. Those
Anglicans who traced their religious origins to Unitarianism and
then converted in later life to the more orthodox faith, often felt
greater kinship to the more liberal denomination rather than to
their Anglican faith. The group was often identified by education.
Daventry Academy was founded by Phillip Dodderige in 1729 as a
school for the Presbyterian ministry, but when it reopened in 1752
with a more Arian orientation Priestley became its first student.[33]
When he joined Warrington Academy in 1761, he was one of four
tutors, all of whom professed Arianism. In the 1820s, Unitarians

founded London University in cooperation with the Utilitarians. In the nineteenth century, Manchester College was almost alone in training Unitarian clergy, while Oxford and Cambridge continued to provide the formal foundation for Anglican faith. The Anglican viewpoint was represented by Frederick Maurice, who had turned from Unitarianism to become a noted Anglican minister. David Young ably expresses the theology of Maurice, centered on the concept that God is the father of the universe and mankind.[34] Other converts from Unitarianism to the Anglican Church included Samuel Taylor Coleridge and William Wordsworth. The Anglican Julius Hare, who freely accepted Unitarians as Christians, was a lecturer at Cambridge and became a close friend of Maurice.[35] Hare was an exception in an Anglican community that had rejected the Unitarian faith, and the liberal outlook of the group of converts caused them to establish closer ties to Unitarians than to Anglicans.

From the Baptist community came Robert Asplund, a young man who had abandoned any hope of the ministry. In 1801 he was appointed minister to the General Baptist congregation of Newport on the Isle of Wight. Four years later he led the Presbyterian New Gravel Pit Chapel at Hackney, formerly occupied by Priestley and Belsham. In 1806 he founded the first Unitarian publication, the Monthly Repository. [36] Theologically Asplund adhered to the more orthodox version of Unitarianism more akin to Christianity and Priestley's Socinianism. Yet he represented the denomination in Parliament and spoke out for religious tolerance. Among his achievements were the organization of the British and Foreign Unitarian Association and the transformation of his publication to the Christian Examiner. His work was continued by his son Robert Brook Asplund, who joined him at the Hackney Chapel and took over the ministry when his father died in 1845. The younger Asplund had been educated at Manchester College and religiously was more akin to Priestley. Another graduate was James Martineau, whom Alan Ruston called a "Bible Based Unitarian." When the denomination came close to a split over theology, pitting Christian Unitarians against Martineau's more liberal beliefs, Asplund fashioned a compromise that preserved the association.[37]

As a young man Martineau's parents had apprenticed him to a

civil engineer in Derby. It was there that he felt the call to the ministry and decided to attend Manchester College. He was influenced by Charles Wellbeloved, a Unitarian minister who taught theology, and John Kendrick, who was dubbed to be totally "devoid of either vanity or dogma."[38] Martineau graduated in 1827 to become a prolific writer and sermonizer. In 1825, while still a student, he delivered the oration: *The Necessity of Cultivating the Imagination as a Regulator of the Devotional Feelings.* His biography appeared in the 1911 issue of the Encyclopedia Britannica and was the subject of a paper by Frank Schulman:

> For a year after graduation Martineau was instructor at Carpenter's school in Bristol. Then he was ordained and called as assistant pastor to the Unitarian Chapel in Dublin, Ireland. He married Helen Higginson, daughter of the Unitarian minister, Edward Higginson, in whose Derby household he had earlier boarded. When Martineau's superior died in 1831 he was entitled to the *regium donum*, a benefit of the crown awarded to Irish dissenting ministers to be given specifically to Presbyterians. He refused it on the grounds that it was perpetrating a religious monopoly "to which the whole nation at large contributes" and had to resign. A few months later he began a twenty-five year ministry at Paradise Street Chapel (later Hope Street Church) in Liverpool.[39]

According to Schulman, Martineau's theology was based on three factors: the moral law, human conscience, and the nature of God. Martineau believed that morality was fundamentally a human trait governed by biblical and legal rules; without these one could not discern how to live one's life. Yet he also believed that humans were able to interpret the Bible only by applying conscience as an arbiter of actions. He directly attributed this feeling to a very personal God. Quoting Schulman, "We are not alone in a cold and friendless world; God is with us and numbers the very hairs on our head. God deals with us individually. Nor do we rely on a God that spake of old. God still speaks if we will listen…"[40] The importance of Martineau to British Unitarianism cannot be underrated. He was to Asplund and Lindsey as Emerson and Parker were to Channing, providing a transcendental alternative to Christian Unitarianism. In his essay on the Christian Student Martineau asked, "What indeed is true theology? It is the knowledge of God. By its very definition therefore it must be co-extensive with the fields of his manifestations, and have something to learn and report wherever his trace has been left...He is Agent and Disposer in outward Nature. He communes with the inmost individual soul. He is the Providence of Collective Humanity..."[41] Martineau maintained that the first task was to find the religious interpretation of the physical sciences, to conceive the meaning of natural laws, and to relate how they interface with God's causality. The second task was to determine the relation of the individual soul to the divine power in order to explain how the free human personality is thrown into "the sweeping tides of pantheistic power."[42] He insisted that ministers must know what they mean when they speak of Will, Conscience, and Reason. The third and last task was to unravel what was meant by divine revelation, specifically questioning the Protestant interpretation of religion as an all-pervasive influence in human affairs. In posing these questions, Martineau moved further away from the facile, dogmatic preaching of orthodox Christianity and its evangelical extension. He began to preach a more modern faith in which man must determine how to live his life. Life was thus oriented to the present, not the hereafter. While such a theology might have appealed to the intellectual bent of the well-educated Unitarian and liberal Anglican, it would become difficult for the orthodox High Churchman and the evangelical dissenter to accept it.

The Christian Socialist movement brought Anglican Frederick Maurice to even closer contact with Unitarians, particularly since his 1838 work, *The Kingdom of God*, recognized the positive aspects of Unitarianism. While the work brought him much recognition, it also relegated him to the left fringe of the Anglican movement.[43] From that vantage Maurice maintained a close association with Unitarians, though he never accepted one of their pulpits and would not preach in their churches. He did, however, admit them to Anglican communion. One of his close associates was Unitarian minister Henry Solly. Also a member of the Christian Socialists,

Solly had addressed in particular the needs of working men. While he recognized their material needs, he also stressed their need for a healthy social environment, deploring their alcoholism and pointing out that the Mechanics Institutes were poorly attended while the Public Houses were full. Solly advocated recreation facilities to replace the pubs, thus combining recreation with education.[44] Equally important was Maurice's friendship with James Martineau and John Llewellyn Davies, the latter an ardent Christian Socialist and an enthusiastic champion of education for women.[45] Elizabeth Gaskell was notable among Unitarian women influenced by Martineau.

While not a part of the Evangelical movement of the orthodox denominations, at the beginning of the nineteenth century Unitarians in England were among the leaders of dissent in their attempts to raise the social conscience of the British population. This mission, to improve the life of all people, was also a characteristic of William Greenleaf Eliot, the first minister of the Unitarian church in Saint Louis. Unitarian congregations continued to practice social action in the late nineteenth and twentieth century, since the Industrial Revolution stirred the conscience of many Unitarians. Raymond Holt claims that, until the middle of the century, Manchester in particular was an unhealthy place for workers, with life spans seventeen years shorter compared to the rest of the country. He maintains that the first generation of mill owners was unsympathetic to social improvement; it was their sons who worked to improve the factory hand's lot.[46] Holt quotes a letter from a Unitarian minister, Charles Kingsley of Manchester, to J. A. Nichols, discussing the undesirability of strikes. Kingsley classified mill owners as nouveau riche and identified the second generation as "the better type", generally Unitarians.[47] They believed in Lord Brougham's attempt at ending slavery, read the Edinburgh Review, and "hated church rates, Orders in Council, the Income Tax, and Corn Laws."[48] A number of industrialists were Unitarians, and the record shows them to be more enterprising and inventive than their orthodox dissenting religionists. Holt cites as examples William Strutt, who made a number of significant improvements to the automatic weaving machine,[49] and Josiah Wedgwood, who founded the modern pottery industry while spawning a number of Unitarian-owned enterprises around his works.[50] Finance was another area where Unitarians made their mark. According to Michael Watts, the Unitarian Heyward Brothers and John Jones founded the major Birmingham banks. Jones married a Unitarian and merged his institution with the Westminster Bank, a major banking force even today.[51]

A friend of Channing, Joseph Tuckerman, had ministered to the poor in Boston and originated the casework method of evaluating the needs of the poor. In 1834 he came to England to encourage Unitarian missionary activities.[52] Webb highlights the special domestic missionaries, who came to the slums of the towns and helped to relieve the burdens of the poor. The Priestley faction concentrated on education, founding schools, universities, mechanics institutes, and libraries, while followers of a new Unitarian group led by Martineau stressed the need for volunteer work.[53] A Unitarian minister and physician, Southwood Smith, campaigned for a safe water supply and for replacing open sewers. Unitarians actively lobbied for the Reform Bill of 1832 and championed anti-slavery legislation. John Fielden, a Member of Parliament from 1832 to 1847, came from a Quaker family but turned to Unitarianism. In Parliament he fought for shorter working hours and laws regulating child labor. In 1847, it resulted in the passage of the Ten Hours Bill, primarily through his efforts. Fielden also opposed the Poor Law Bill, and he worked to change the tax system from one based on consumption to one based on property.[54] Elizabeth Gaskell, daughter of a Unitarian and wife to a Unitarian minister, wrote novels exposing the clash between hardhearted mill owners and their impoverished weavers.[55] Unitarians were very active in advocating social reforms, but by the 1830s Evangelicals such as Edward Irving and Henry Drummond became "fiercely hostile to co-operation with Unitarians."[56] In 1836, Unitarians were forced out of the General Body of Protestant Dissenting Ministers. Their social involvement continued but no longer as a part of general dissent.

The era from 1833 to 1834 was a highly productive period for reform legislation. Slavery was abolished in Britain, and a bill regulating child labor was passed, as was a compromise Irish Church Bill by which Irish Catholics could worship freely along those who professed Anglican beliefs. The other major accomplishment was a revision of the Poor Law that enabled paupers to escape the burden of the Poor House. Another Unitarian reform initiative was tax relief. For decades a major bone of contention had been a levy placed on all for the support of the Anglican Church, the so-called *church rates*. The drive to abolish this tax ran into stubborn church opposition and died in the House of Commons. During this period Charles Dickens, a Unitarian and prolific author, began to publish first short stories and later novels dealing with the plight of the poor and those caught by the vagaries of the British Common Law. His popularity grew, and his influence on social issues was felt throughout the long reign of Queen Victoria (1837–1901).

While Unitarians and Anglicans worked together to improve the social condition of the working classes, their theological orientation remained apart, though under the influence of James Martineau, they shared an aversion to growing sectarianism in England.[57] In the first decades of the nineteenth century, Unitarian theology experienced a split into two conflicting views, one championed by radical Joseph Priestley and the other by moderate Martineau. Priestley, through fifteen volumes of his works, firmly annunciated a single vision of Unitarian faith. His fourth volume dealt with church history. While covering in great detail the workings of the various church councils, including the Council of Nicea, he concluded with an analysis of why the Trinity had not been accepted by the early Christians. He based his argument on the gospel according to Mark, written earliest and perhaps the only one by an apostle who actually knew Christ. Priestley pointed out, like others before him, that there was no mention of a divine Jesus in the gospel, nor could the final discovery of the empty tomb by the women be interpreted as an act of resurrection.[58] From the Anglican standpoint such a theology was heresy, but, according to Young, the teachings of toleration, social progress, and personal liberty made Priestley's work acceptable to both Michael Maurice and his son Frederick. It became the fundamental philosophical underpinning of the Christian Socialists.[59]

Since Priestley could relate to the Anglicans only on social issues, Martineau modified Priestley's rigid theology and combined it with the views of liberal Anglicans to create a less doctrinaire theology. Per Watts, Charles Jerram, an Anglican minister, stated that "Unitarian sermons were mere moral essays, philosophical disquisitions and refined in style. They contained no appeal to conscience...no consolation to the afflicted."[60] He was speaking about the followers of Priestley and perhaps sensed the modern trend of the Unitarian Church. Orthodox Anglicans and dissenters attacked Unitarianism unmercifully, and one of Wesley's hymns reads: "Stretch out thine arm oh Triune God ! The Unitarian fiend expel, And chase his doctrines back to Hell."[61] Yet Maurice's preaching incorporated much of the permissive Unitarian theology, differing primarily in the central point of Christ's divinity. When he persuaded Joseph Hutton, Unitarian minister at Gloucester, to turn to the Anglican Church, he achieved only a partial conversion. Hutton still maintained that Christ, while divine, had a subservient role to the Father.[62] Both Martineau and Maurice actively espoused doctrines that were closely aligned, a fact that enabled the English Unitarian Church to grow.

One of the remarkable qualities of the British Unitarian movement was the dedication of Unitarian women to social and political reform. Kathryn Gleadle, who has addressed Unitarian feminism, maintains that it was natural that Unitarians were generally sympathetic to "advanced ideas of womanhood."[63] William Shepherd had advocated female suffrage as early as 1790. However, the mores of the times, especially those restricting females to the home, were still being practiced by the more conservative Unitarian industrialists. The Courtauld silk mills employed women in manual capacities, generally from the laboring classes. Manchester mill owners, many of whom were Unitarian, believed in a patriarchal system. In Liverpool, a hotbed of Unitarian industrial owners, the Rathbone family encouraged female learning and intellectual pursuits, particularly advocating for their education. William Rathbone joined other Unitarians to form the Roscoe Club, and crafted a charter allowing it to admit women, however, their attendance was discouraged. According to Gleadle the Rathbones attended the services of the radical Unitarian William Johnson Fox.[64] Fox intensively espoused feminist causes in the Monthly Repository, and he advocated fair employment practices. His colleagues, J. B. Estlin and lawyer William Shean, restricted themselves to advocating for the education of women. Fox himself attracted a veritable Who's Who in British literary life to his South Place Chapel. People like Bulwer Lytton, John Forster, Charles Dickens and Robert Browning were joined by John Stuart Mills and Harriet Taylor.[65] The novelist Mary Wollestonecraft, daughter of the radical feminist of the same name, was also part of the circle.

But more important was the Unitarian support of the Chartist movement in the mid-1830s. Chartists were laborers who petitioned Parliament for their rights –the Chart. They were familiar with the United States Declaration of Independence, had lived through two French revolutions in 1789 and 1830, and were discouraged by the British Reform Act of 1832, believing that it did not go far enough. Chartists wanted universal suffrage, the secret ballot, annual parliaments, and pay for members of parliament so that even middle-class men could stand for the positions. Unitarian industrialist such as Samuel Courtauld belonged to the Radical Club, as did many who supported the Owenite movement, a nineteenth century experiment in industrial socialism by Robert Owen. Yet Unitarians, to the chagrin of orthodox Chartists, demanded extension of the franchise to women. Women like Harriet Taylor wrote articles and books supporting this, as did Cathryn and Goodwin Barnaby. They demanded women's suffrage in the name of Mary Wollstonecraft and Charlotte Corday. The leaders of the Chartist movement despised these attempts to extend suffrage, and Faergus O'Connor, a leading Chartist, bitterly denounced them. It was the beginning of the participation of the Unitarian movement in the British suffragette campaign for the vote. Articles in Unitarian publications strongly supported their position, as did Unitarian ministers.

In spite of attacks by orthodoxy and after an initial decline, Unitarian churches in England started to grow significantly in the last decade of the eighteenth century. In London, where there had only been two churches in 1789, there were twenty in 1810.[66] Short points out that the nature of the London congregation changed. Most Unitarians were now professionals who "valued Unitarianism as a banner of enlightenment."[67] Some were members of Parliament, fifteen in the House of Commons in 1834.[68] During the 1820s the denomination started its own publications, the Monthly Repository later to become the Christian Reformer and a book society to publish Unitarian tracts. In 1826, Richard Wright, Robert Brook Asplund, and William Johnson Fox organized the British and Foreign Unitarian Association. In 1851 there were 229 Unitarian churches in England and Wales with an attendance of 33,000 as compared to 2,789 Baptist and 3,244 Congregational chapels.[69] Unitarianism was clearly not accepted by the majority of churchgoers, but it had grown in numbers and even more so in influence. Manchester College had become the training ground for the Unitarian ministry. It moved from Manchester to York in 1803 and back to Manchester in 1840. In 1853 it moved to London and in 1889 to Oxford.

In 1835, Martineau had started to preach the new, more liberal Unitarianism. He was joined in this by J. H. Thom and Charles Wickstead. These ministers abandoned the Priestley tenet of biblical Christianity and rationalism for a theology more akin to romanticism. Others like Southwood Smith, Fox, and Robert Asplund stuck to the Priestley version of Unitarianism. The difference was that the Martineau faction in the late 1830s was more devout and Christ centered than Priestley and Lindsey. While they retained the concept of a human Christ, they were ready to love him "in meek faith and trust."[70] Yet Martineau became convinced that religion also had to address the everyday problems of life, and he turned his attention to social conditions.[71] His view would direct the denomination away from a preoccupation with the hereafter to a ministry that tried to persuade people that God's will was to live a moral life on earth. In his essay *The Crisis of Faith*, he clearly defined the problems of orthodox theology, problems that Unitarians did not face when they expressed their beliefs. His primary argument was that the concept of Jesus' atonement for mankind's sins was illogical. In his discussion he dealt with the absurdity of God creating an innocent being yet imposing on him at birth a burden of mortal sin. He called this an attempt by the conventional churches to frighten people with images of terror.[72] The incarnation, Martineau asserted, could not be discovered by any but supernatural means, calling it "an event belonging to two worlds, involving in both exceptional phenomena beyond the range of observation and testimony."[73] As for the gospels, he pointed out their conflicting views of the nature of Jesus and attributed this to the fact that they were written by men, none of whom really knew him. He was well aware of the contradictory evidence of science, maintaining that science "traces finite causation till it is lost in the infinite," while religion is "an infinite cause till it appears in the finite."[74] Yet Martineau was also a staunch advocate of the separation of church and state. In his essay titled *The Battle of the Churches*, he discusses primarily the Catholic and Anglican denominations' struggle for supremacy. With strong faith in the ability of reasoning people to reject orthodox religion, he opposed parliamentary action to curb the established church:

> With our eye, then, full upon the inevitable tendencies of the Romish system; with the conviction that it generates a state of mind at variance with the English standard of civil and religious liberty; with the certain knowledge , that the equal and tolerant treatment it receives it will never, in its place and day of power, be willing to reciprocate,- we yet say to our fellow-countrymen, Be just and fear not; put not your trust in coercive laws…The free mind and the large heart, in yourselves and your children, will be a surer charm against the priest and the canon law, than preventive statutes or an outcry for the Queen's supremacy.[75]

By 1838 the differences between those who adhered to Priestley's Unitarianism and those who believed in the reasoned and compromising approach of Martineau had split the movement. Robert Webb analyzed Martineau's famous sermon, *The Bible, What it is and What it is Not* and identified this as a new theology, in it Martineau rejected the concept of infallibility and ranked the books of the New Testament in order of authority. As for miracles, he admitted that a Christian could reject them all but was then faced with the need to explain creation. He felt that Christ might have inspired the apostles to imagine the miracles of the Bible, but whether or not they were true was of little consequence.[76] He identified all religions as supernatural and felt that any believer could accept or reject the gospels as truth, but he also felt that the supreme authority for man had to be reason.[77] His theology paralleled American Unitarian Ralph Waldo Emerson's transcendentalism.

In 1838, a meeting of Unitarians in London discussed the split and called for greater cooperation between the two factions. While no general conclusions could be reached, there appeared a consensus that the eighteenth century foundation of Unitarianism was eroding. Or, as Wilbur put it, Unitarianism founded on ancient history and relying on external authority would give way to the inner conviction of man.[78] Martineau continued to be controversial, and preaching that the Unitarian name should only identify an individual's faith but should not be used for the whole denomination. His sermons began to depend less and less on biblical thought, thereby paralleling the American movement of Theodore Parker. This period also saw the abandonment of the simple chapel concept for Unitarian churches in favor of the traditional Gothic style used by orthodox denominations. While the initial decision to change was based on economics (Michael Watts pointed out that gothic glass was cheaper than Greek stone), another major factor seems to have been the desire of Unitarians to demonstrate visually that their religion was as respectable as that preached in the Anglican gothic churches.[79] In 1866 an attempt was made to adopt an official Unitarian doctrine as to God and Christ, but this was overwhelmingly rejected. From this point on Unitarians increasingly abandoned any requirement of a uniform faith, and today's beliefs ranging from a total theism to a total humanism come from this period.

Unitarians of the nineteenth century were activists, belonging to the Whig and later the Liberal Party. They had become active in politics in the last decade of the eighteenth century, and several led the move towards reform. William Smith was a powerful Member of Parliament who fought alongside the evangelical Wilberforce for the abolition of slavery, an effort that in 1833 was successful in outlawing the practice for Britain and its possessions. He was also instrumental in passing the ten hour act, the limitation on child and women labor. Watts names eleven Unitarian members of parliament active around the turn of the century but is careful to point out that several, such as Benjamin Hobhouse and Robert Wigram, maintained their ties to the Anglican Church, while one of them, John C. Hobhouse, son of Benjamin and also a member of parliament, was a Unitarian favoring repeal.[80] Two cabinet members assisted in passing reform legislation, Lord John Russell, who became prime minister, though he too maintained his Anglican affiliation, and Joseph Chamberlain, later colonial secretary and an openly active Unitarian.

Tensions arose between the Unitarians and the Presbyterians in the 1840s. Presbyterians had brought suit against Unitarians for using church property that was willed to congregations when they were still Trinitarian. In one particular instance, the Lady Hewley's charity called for the return of a Birmingham chapel that had a long history of Unitarian use but when originally endowed was Presbyterian. In the ensuing court case, adjudicated in 1842, the ruling went against Unitarians and they were denied legal rights to the property. With some two hundred existing Unitarian churches could be similarly ordered to vacate their property, church attendance dropped, as congregations lost confidence in the long-term viability of the movement. It required an act of parliament, passed in July 1844, to reverse the court ruling, allowing Unitarians to keep property that had been in their possession for more than twenty-five years.[81]

Another major issue fervently espoused by Unitarians was the reform of parliamentary representation. The early1800s were the heyday of "rotten boroughs," those with very few people yet had representation by a member of parliament. Also a large number of rural districts were represented compared to those of growing cities. This was addressed by the famous Reform Act of 1832, which provided ninety-four more seats in parliament, mostly allocated to towns. In the post-reform 1832 election, nine Unitarians entered parliament as compared to the Wesleyan and Primitive Wesleyans, the Congregationalists, and Baptists, who elected no members.[82]

Joseph Chamberlain was perhaps typical of the political involvement of Unitarian reformers. He was born in London in 1836, one of eight children. His parents were in trade and devout Unitarians.[83] Chamberlain was educated in the University College School, popular with Unitarians because of its non-sectarian character. He founded the Club for Workingmen and the Birmingham Educational Society, became mayor of Birmingham, was elected to parliament, and ultimately colonial secretary.[84] Peter Marsh maintained that Chamberlain's Unitarianism was based on the rational beliefs of Priestley, sharpening his capacity for social analysis.[85] Chamberlain's political and social orientation was revealed in an 1873 article, where he linked additional parliamentary reform with freedom for dissenting religion and the provision of non-sectarian education. He deplored a split in the Liberal Party, which caused enough liberals to vote with conservatives to defeat reforms beyond the 1867 Act, and pointed out that the Liberal Party was the party of dissent. It needed to unite behind a slogan "Free Church, Free Land, Free Schools, Free Labour."[86]

In the 1860s, as the second Reform Bill was being debated, it appeared that Tories would belong to the Church of England while Liberals drew heavily from the ranks of dissent. Viscount Amberley, son of Lord John Russell, a member of parliament and a Unitarian at least by persuasion, argued for greater tolerance by the Anglican Church in a paper titled *Liberals, Conservatives and the Church*.[87] He described the Tory position as uncompromising in every sense. On the other hand, Liberals often compromised their fundamental beliefs to "declare that they are warmly attached to the Church of England, yet they favor abolishing church rates and university tests."[88] Amberley ridiculed the conservative stance denying to dissenters burial in consecrated grounds as a feeble attempt to discourage heresy and schism, and remarked that even the inquisition did a better job. He pointed out that there were really only two options. The first required declaring that there is only one true religion, and all who did not follow it risked eternal damnation and thus could not be buried in existing cemeteries. Such a position would have to be enforced by the state. The second was that man was responsible for his own beliefs and to his own conscience, not for the beliefs of his fellow creatures, and thus was free to act even in death. This was the Unitarian view, and Amberley expressed the hope that this rationale would eventually be used for the establishment of a National Church, one that could include a Theodore Parker, a Ralph Waldo Emerson and a Francis Newman. He stated that the absence of a creed would accommodate the Unitarians, "who have as good a claim to a place within a National Church as any other sect."[89]

Unitarians of the nineteenth century were considered part of the mainstream of dissent, as were their Presbyterian antecedents, but their prominence in English cultural life did not necessarily endear them to the conventional evangelical, a bias that seems to have been carried over to modern times. The rational theology of the denomination has been classed by various authors as sterile or arid,[90] and in 1995, Donald Davie, a Cambridge University faculty member, resurrected this conclusion, writing:

> It could be argued, and with justice, that the Unitarians have, in proportion to their numbers and their relatively brief history(sic), made a greater contribution to English culture than all the other dissenting sects put together. Certainly this would be plausible if we proceeded simply by counting heads, enumerating the distinguished individuals who have emerged from among the Unitarians to contribute to the intellectual life of the nation. But, much as we must guard against any sentimentally populist understanding of 'culture', it is undeniable that Unitarians seem in almost every generation to have regarded themselves as an intellectual *elite*, 'gathered' from the world more self-consciously and haughtily than even those other sects which were surest of being 'the elect'.[91]

He then proceeds to describe the Salter's Hall vote as a Unitarian takeover and classes the 1772 attempt to amend the Toleration Act as the work of "Unitarians masquerading as Presbyterians," a rather strange comment since many Presbyterians of that time openly held Unitarian views. Davie then addresses Unitarian literary accomplishments and describes Elizabeth Gaskell as dealing compassionately with "the scandalous topic of the unmarried mother" in her novel *Ruth*, and classes the minister, who is the hero of the novel, as far removed from "all the cursing evangelicals." While Davie admits that the North West Midland Unitarians were strong, he adds Norwich as another center with "the most elegant meeting house in England" and describes Harriet Martineau as "an even more famous Unitarian bluestocking." Norwich was also the home of William Hale White, a Unitarian and author of *The Autobiography of Mark Rutherford*, a work that Davie calls even more sterile than the products of orthodox dissent. He then proceeds to damn by faint praise Unitarian cultural accomplishments, objecting to an orientation favoring speculative thought and ideas over those of images and dubbing the cultural contributions as having "propagandist intentions."[92] Ultimately he finds little in Unitarian literature that compares to the "great novelists in the sense of George Eliot or Charles Dickens or Emily Brontë," and dismisses Unitarian contributions through the ages as having a constricted imagination and suffering from timidity.

It is then refreshing to read an excerpt from Mrs. Gaskell's work, hardly sterile, describing a Unitarian congregation of rural Cheshire:

> The congregation consisted of here and there a farmer and his labourers, who came down from the uplands behind the town to worship where their fathers worshipped, and who loved the place because they knew how much their fathers had suffered for it, although they never troubled themselves with the reason why they left the parish church; and of a few shopkeepers, far more thoughtful and reasoning, who were dissenters from conviction…With many poor, who were drawn there by love for Mr. Benson's character [the minister], and by feeling that the faith which made him what he was could not be far wrong…[93]

Robert Webb identifies Mrs. Gaskell as a Unitarian whose faith can be summed up by terms like liberal, humanitarian, or even Christian, thus countering any attempt to evict her from the mainstream of Victorian religious life.[94] In the introduction to their volume of documents on dissent, John Briggs and Ian Sellers recognize that orthodox Christianity had portrayed dissenters as "ignorant, drab, provincial and depressing" and tried to dismiss them from the Victorian religious scene. To counter that, they quote Lord John Russell, who pointed out that dissenters were responsible for passing the reform bill, abolishing slavery, favoring free trade, and were willing to abolish church rates. He classed their championship of these issues as a crucial contribution to the making of Victorian England.[95]

By 1865, as Martineau continued to redefine Priestley's Necessarian concepts of Unitarianism, it became clear that what Webb calls the protracted crisis of English Unitarianism needed to be resolved.[96] The question was whether the teachings of Priestley were still valid and relevant as an expression of Unitarian faith, or whether Martineau's approach of a less sectarian Unitarianism based more on free will should be adopted. That issue had divided the movement, since many churches in England and abroad rejected Priestley's affirmation of the sole divinity of God the Father and the restoration of soul and body in the hereafter. He had also preached that God had foreknowledge of all events, and therefore was as much responsible for man's evil as for good, a thesis that he used to justify the belief in God's acceptance of all mortals into heaven. Priestley had also rejected the Calvinist notion of a judgmental God for one who "was infinitely benevolent, a judge who only issued interlocutory decrees."[97] Countering this was Martineau, who believed in human free will and the role of conscience in man's religious life. Yet his theology had evolved into a more theistic mode, though it denied miracles, and approached a science- based, natural, non-judgmental religion. His biography in the 1911 Encyclopedia Britannica attributes to him a reverent approach to the teachings of Jesus, human but divinely inspired. He stressed the need for a moral life on earth and doubted the concept of life after death. Resolution of this divide was achieved in the United States by William Ellery Channing who bridged factions, and his philosophy, heavily Christian and closer to Martineau's acceptance of free will, was also accepted by English Unitarians. As Webb puts it, "his warm eloquence appealed to a generation no longer satisfied with the style of eighteenth century preaching and devotion." Simultaneously Unitarianism became the home of social and political reform. It shared that mission with liberal Anglicans, particularly in the Christian Socialist movement. The close cooperation between the two denominations, so far apart in doctrine, can be traced to Martineau's and Maurice's shared view of Christian responsibility for improving life on earth (even as they could never agree on Christ's role as a savior).

The British reform movement was witness to the inordinate influence of a minority sect in the country's social and political life. The fifty thousand mid-nineteenth century British Unitarians indeed "weighed more than they measured,"[98] but they did so by social position, alliances with liberal Anglicans, and espousal of popular causes. In 1912 England there were nearly four hundred active Unitarian churches, mostly small congregations consisting primarily of working people. For over seventy years, however, there had existed an active missionary movement to found new churches and to support the existing ones. This was successful. The real Unitarian miracle was that the denomination remained a viable religious force despite of doctrinaire differences, and that it accomplished so much.

CHAPTER 2:

From Boston To the West
The Development of American Unitarianism

During the seventeenth century, religion was brought to the thirteen colonies from England by settlers who often based their faith on the dogma of an Anglican Church that was dominant, and preached a most unforgiving brand of Calvinism. That was not true of the pilgrims, whose puritan theology emphasized that sin dominated human actions. Having left England for Holland to escape the rigor of Anglicanism, the pilgrims fashioned a covenant describing a Christianity unsullied by outside influences. Anglican settlers established a congregational polity only loosely controlled by the Church of England but filled with Calvinist concepts of original sin, election, and predestination. Neither, however, made many attempts to appeal to the emotions. At the same time, the Puritans in Massachusetts, under the leadership of Cotton Mather, then pastor of Boston's North Church, were afflicted with the belief in witches. In 1692, he presided over witchcraft trials in Salem and condemned to death many who opposed him. In 1722, he raised the alarm that New England ministers were not preaching the divinity of Christ. This was true, since, as the eighteenth century began, some began to doubt the concept of the Trinity and express Arminian views. By 1734, with Mather discredited, a revival movement, the Great Awakening, swept across the colonies led by Jonathan

Edwards. Abandoning the ritual of the established churches, he preached about sinful man and human redemption by confession and baptism, and he fanned emotions by highlighting the terrors of hellfire and damnation. He generated great excitement, but at the same time he left many deeply questioning the dogmatic way in which Puritans and Anglicans had characterized religion. His zeal motivated Arminians that preached a loving God to greater action. James Freeman, who became minister of Boston's King's Chapel in 1786, particularly opposed the revivalist's view of salvation. By 1750, over thirty ministers had abandoned Calvinism, and there was reason to think that the orthodox Anglican movement was in danger.[99] It was the beginning of the growth of Unitarianism in New England churches.

While Earl Morse Wilbur dismissed any transfusion of religious thought between England and America, this was very limited. He states:

> Nothing would be more natural at find American Unitarianism merely a transplantation into a fresh field of a religion already fully developed and organized by the colonists that settled New England in other countries…Such an expectation, however first thought than to expect that here we should, would not be confirmed by the facts; for there is no evidence that the Socinianism of the continent had more than the slightest influence, if any, on the development of Unitarianism in America, or that Socinian books were known or read in New England by any one at the time when Unitarianism was first taking shape there. Still less can Unitarianism in Massachusetts be accounted for as something brought over from England in the seventeenth century, for at that period the Unitarian movement had not yet arisen in England. Nor even when the Unitarian movement was becoming coherent here were there more than two or three places…in which there was any direct influence exercised by leaders of

the Unitarian movement at the end of the eighteenth century...[100]

Yet by the end of the eighteenth century, Thomas Belsham and Joseph Priestley, both English Unitarian ministers, were in the United States, and Ellery Channing would travel to England in 1822. American Unitarians were well aware of the Socinian strains of the English churches, since there was frequent correspondence between New England and English Unitarian clerics. Priestley, for one, actively preached Socianism and persuaded President Jefferson to adopt the Unitarian faith. He also travelled throughout the Eastern states trying to establish Unitarian churches, and went as far west as Ohio. At the same time, New England Unitarians were Arians, led by those trained at the Harvard Divinity School. Originally, those that adopted the Unitarian name generally rejected the English view that Jesus was merely a prophet. Their theology reflected a strong Arminian strain, and they abandoned the concepts of original sin passed to all mankind and predestination. They asserted that Christ was divine but subordinate to God. It was inconceivable to those preaching a loving God that he would condemn vast numbers of humanity to everlasting damnation, despite Jonathan Edwards preaching. As Conrad Wright put it: "[The liberal movement in theology] …rejected the concept of human nature as totally corrupt and depraved and supplanted it with one in which the ability of every man to strive for righteousness was admitted."[101]   Indeed American ministers that professed doubt in Christ's divinity during the eighteenth century did so initially as a rejection of the orthodox Calvinist views of original sin. By the mid-eighteenth century, those that held Arian views came under intense attack by conservative Trinitarians. The battle centered in New England, Yale University defending traditional Calvinism and Harvard tolerating liberal dissent.

In 1755, the controversy burst into the open when Jonathan Mayhew questioned the Trinity. He was minister of Boston's West Church and an overseer of Harvard University. Mayhew was joined in his Arian viewpoint by Ebenezer Gay, minister of the Hingham church, and Charles Chauncy, minister of Boston's First Church. These men would not accept the appellation *Arian*, but clearly annunciated the lesser status of Jesus. It fell to James Freeman, who became minister at King's Chapel in 1783, and William Bentley, who came to Salem's East Church at the same time, to advocate Socinian views, in spite of the professed Anglican orientation of their parishes. Two years later, a member of King's Chapel, Colonel Joseph May, was instrumental in removing Trinitarian references from its liturgy. He became an assistant church warden in 1795 and held that position until 1826. His son Samuel would also become a Unitarian minister. Thus a spectrum of beliefs was heard from clerics in the Boston area who accepted the name Unitarian. Yet, according to George E. Ellis, then a professor at the Harvard Divinity School, many others held Unitarian beliefs but were loath to abandon their Congregational or Episcopal churches, because they had "an intense dislike to sectarian strife, to party organizations in religion, and to the working of all agencies requisite for such enterprises."[102] He then distinguished orthodox theology from liberal theology in a number of ways. Orthodoxy accepted the Calvinist interpretation of Christianity, the thirty-two articles of faith, and worshipped the triune God, Father, Son and Holy Ghost. Liberals rejected this and believed in the "undivided unity of the Supreme Being."[103] This of course required an Armenian reinterpretation of the gospels and rejection of beliefs in original sin, election, and the role of atonement. Yet even amid revivals and the preaching of hellfire and damnation by orthodoxy, the liberal religion became established in the new republic. Perhaps the thrust for political freedom automatically engendered liberality in religion. Thus many early political figures of the young nation accepted Unitarian views. They might attend churches Congregational in name, but their religion was Arian in outlook. Thomas Jefferson, Benjamin Franklin, John Adams, and John Quincy Adams all were Unitarians.

It should have been evident to the advocates of liberal alternatives to Calvinism that their views would be strenuously opposed. The resultant public discussion began to peak in the first decade of the nineteenth century and became known as the Unitarian Controversy. Most of New England continued to proclaim traditional Christian Trinitarian and Calvinist beliefs. In Boston and its surroundings, however, increasing numbers of churches called liberal ministers to their pulpits, amply supplied by Harvard. The first and fundamental controversy was a public comparison of Unitarianism with the precepts of orthodoxy. Only later, in the 1830s, a different argument arose, but this time all within the Unitarian movement. It split the denomination between those that were Unitarian Christians and those who questioned the validity of the gospels and its miracles.

At the center of the first controversy was William Ellery Channing. He entered Harvard in 1794, and, when he graduated, was determined to become a minister. It took seven years, however, for him to return to Harvard for graduate work in divinity. In 1802 he received his license to preach, and during his first engagements at the First Church of Medford, he was deemed to be a moderate Calvinist.[104] An important feature of Boston area's religious life was the ability of ministers to exchange pulpits. It was implicit in an invitation for exchange that the theology of the visitor match the religious views of the settled minister, though modest excursions from established views were accepted. Thus Channing was invited to preach at the Federal Street church and the Brattle Street congregation. The young minister made a good impression and soon was asked to candidate at both churches. Of the two, Brattle Street was larger and more solidly established, yet Channing felt the smaller Federal Street church was more suitable to his desire to be of personal service to members of the congregation.[105] In June 1803 Channing was ordained and became minister of that church, a position he would hold until his death in 1842. During that time Unitarianism in New England directly opposed the Calvinist theology, deemed to be mainline Christian. Channing had begun to deviate from orthodoxy and was instead advancing a more liberal interpretation of Christ's role. In April 1815, he preached at the ordination of John Abbott at the Salem church. Madeleine Rice highlights his new orientation, a warning against concentrating on the personality of Christ as opposed to the teachings of Christ.[106] The Unitarian controversy, as it was called, came to a head in 1805, when Henry Ware, a liberal theologian, was appointed to the Hollis chair of divinity at Harvard and put the school squarely into the Unitarian column. Jebediah Morse defended Orthodox Christianity in an article in the Panoplist Review, in which he decried the spread of Unitarianism. In order to highlight the danger of the liberal theology, Morse used the writings of Thomas Belsham, then visiting the United States, with his decided Socinian views of Christ as mere man. Morse maintained that Unitarians had accepted the catechism of Theophilus Lindsay:

> There is nation, one God, one single person who is God, the sole Creator and Sovereign Lord of all things.
>
> The holy Jesus was a man of the Jewish nation, the servant of this God, highly honored and distinguished by him.
>
> The Spirit, or Holy Spirit, was not a person or intelligent being, but only the extraordinary power or gift of God, first to our Lord Jesus Christ himself in his life time, and afterwards to the apostles and many of the first Christians, to impower them to preach and propagate the Gospel with success."[107]

He concluded that Unitarians were hiding their belief in Jesus as man in order to maintain good relations with Boston churchgoers and clergy. Thus he called them hypocrites and urged them to abandon their heretical ministers. Until they did so, Unitarians should be denied communion. Channing took the lead to rebut this in an open letter to his friend Samuel C. Thatcher, minister of Boston's South Church. First, he rejected the claim that Unitarians accepted the Socinianism of Belsham and Lindsey. He wrote: "We both [he and Thatcher] agreed...that a majority of our brethren believe that Jesus Christ is more than man, that he existed before the world, the he literally came from heaven to save our race, that he sustains other offices than those of a teacher..."[108] Other Unitarians, while they might have difficulty in coming to a precise definition of the nature of Christ, still "rest in the conclusion that he, whom God has appointed to be our Savior, follows him as their Lord". Second, Channing rejected any implication that the majority of Unitarians were not Christians, as Morse implied.

It took four more years for Channing to develop the theology that became known as Unitarian Christianity, which he defined in a sermon preached on May 5, 1819, in the First Independent Church of Baltimore, at the ordination of Jared Sparks. He defined for the American movement the meaning of Unitarianism as the belief "in the doctrine of God's unity, or that there is one God and one only."[109] He cited as proof the absence of any mention of the Trinity in the gospels, nor did he find anything in Judaism that would countenance a belief in a triune God. Channing asserted that, were the gospels to contain references to the Trinity, this would overshadow all other deeds of Jesus and the apostles. He went on to reject the concept of a dual divine and human role for Jesus and insisted that Unitarians believed in the unity of Jesus just as they believed in the unity of God: "It is a great excellence of the doctrine of God's unity that it offers to us one object of supreme homage, adoration and love. One Infinite Father, one Being of beings, one original and fountain, to whom we may refer all good, in whom all our powers and affections may be concentrated, and whose lovely and venerable nature may pervade all our thoughts."[110]

Regarding the Bible, he stated that "[Unitarians] regard the scriptures as the record of God's successive revelation to mankind, and particularly of the last and most perfect revelation of his will by Jesus Christ."[111] He went on to explain that, in interpreting the Bible, Unitarians treated it as a book "written for men in the language of men, and the meaning is to be sought in the same manner as other books."[112] Since it was written by men, even though they were inspired by God, it was a testament to the events of that day, to the status of biblical society, and to the thinking of its authors.[113] Thus the Bible should be subject to the interpretation of men who must look beyond its words to the nature of the subject. He admitted that such a stance was not exclusively Unitarian and that other denominations had the same challenge, but he rejected beliefs that from the fall of Adam and Eve "mysterious doctrines about the divine nature" should be deduced. Channing pointed out that through the ages many errors of biblical interpretation had occurred, most of them by sects that forbade reasoning. He then proceeded to a fundamental Arminian argument: if God is infinitely wise, then he will bring the truth to those that use reason, and will not condemn them. He clearly enunciated the Unitarian view of God's unity, rejecting the concept of "three infinite and equal persons, with their own wills, consciousness and perceptions."[114] He concluded by quoting the Bible: "With Jesus we worship the Father as the only living and true God." Channing addressed the nature of Jesus "as one soul, one mind, one being as truly one as we are, and equally distinct from the one God."[115] He dismissed the concept of Jesus' infinite atonement. and affirmed that "God is infinitely good, kind, benevolent, to every individual and to the general system." The concept of original sin would be totally foreign to such a God. But equally important, Channing addressed the role reason plays in the acceptance of the scriptures. He thus, perhaps unwittingly, laid a philosophical foundation that would soon be used by Ralph Waldo Emerson in formulating transcendentalism and by Theodore Parker in his definition of pure or absolute religion. In contrast to those who insisted on the literal interpretation of the Bible, Channing pleaded for use of reason to sort out the diverse origin of biblical text, its inconsistencies, and its contradictions. Yet he was careful to accept the Bible as an inspired, if not revealed, text and with it the miracles of the New Testament.

It was Ware's professorship that enabled Harvard to provide a broad spectrum of Unitarian philosophy, and to create a theology equally acceptable to both sides. He also was first to establish that Unitarian churches should be open to all beliefs and have no creed:

> Unitarians have always claimed the right of every individual to have his or her view of religion. What they have sometimes objected to is, not that each of the several sects and denominations should have their own creed, nor that any, whether an individual or a body of Christians, should insist upon their particular creed being the creed of others; either as a title to a Christian name, or as a condition of their being admitted to the participation of any Christian privileges.[116]

Daniel Howe described a fundamental question addressed by Ware: "Why should we promote the general good?"[117] His answer was that everyone knew that this was the right thing to do. Unitarians were caught, however, in a constant comparison of revelation and reason, with revelation being faith based and reason reconciled with the view that the world could not have been created by random processes. They were undoubtedly influenced by the British theologian William Paley, who, in his 1802 work *Natural Theology,* made the analogy that were one to find a fine watch in an uninhabited desert, one would have to conclude that it had been made by a skilled watchmaker. Thus, Ware tried to reconcile a supernatural belief in God and his creation with what was then known about nature. This preceded Darwin's *Origins of the Species*, published in 1859, with little acceptance of the work until decades later.

The importance of the Harvard Divinity School in Unitarian history is best illustrated by the timeline of events that defined the denomination. In 1802, Channing entered the Harvard Divinity School, then still a professed moderate Calvinist, and was ordained a year later. He took over the pulpit of Boston's Federal Street Church in 1803, a position he would hold for the rest of his active preaching life. Ware took over Harvard's Hollis chair in 1805. At that time only one Unitarian minister was installed in a Connecticut church. In 1815, Channing actively defended Henry Ware yet still had not formulated his view of Unitarianism. That occurred four years later. In 1818, Samuel Joseph May, son of Joseph May of King's Chapel, entered Harvard Divinity School to become a Unitarian minister. At that time Ralph Waldo Emerson was also a student at Harvard with Channing very much his mentor. In a span of twenty years, one quarter of all Massachusetts Congregational churches turned to Unitarian ministers, while in Connecticut a dozen adopted Unitarian principles. In May 1820, Channing invited all Massachusetts liberal ministers to the vestry of his church (whose entrance was on Berry Street). At the meeting Channing delivered an address. He urged upon his colleagues a "bond of union" among liberal Christian ministers, within which they might meet to exchange practical ideas for strengthening their faith. In order to do so, they established an annual essay series at which a minister could discuss any topic related to the broad aspects of Unitarian theology. By 1830, Unitarian churches were founded in Louisville and Cincinnati with ministers trained at Harvard. In 1831 William Greenleaf Eliot entered the Divinity School. For the next three years he was exposed to the full spectrum of Unitarian thought influenced by Channing and Ware, after which he finally reached Saint Louis is 1834. This also was the year that Theodore Parker entered the school as a junior, graduating in June 1835. Eliot founded the Church of the Messiah in Saint Louis in January 1835, preaching Unitarian Christianity. Emerson made his attack on traditional Unitarianism in his famous Divinity School address in 1838. Parker annunciated his concept of absolute religion in the 1841 sermon *The Transient and the Permanent in Christianity.*

While Boston was the institutional birthplace of United States Unitarianism, the rest of the new nation also began to embrace liberal religion. Joseph Priestley was the evangelist who crisscrossed the west preaching Socinianism from Pennsylvania to Ohio, and Harvard graduates spread Henry Ware's Arianism south from Boston. In major cities of the eastern states Unitarian churches were formed. Also, in the first decades of the nineteenth century, the budding United States began to settle the open country. Settlers brought with them religious beliefs; some were formulated during the Great Awakening and were therefore Calvinist, some were decidedly Arminian. Some settlers came with strong religious faith having left the old country for religious reasons and brought their heritage into the territories. In spite of the fervor of evangelical Calvinism, some ministers felt constrained by the unforgiving punishment promised to unrepentant sinners and turned to a more forgiving faith. Thus they were open to Ballou's Universalism or Priestley's Socinianism, and the Unitarian message began to spread west. Charles Lyttle describes this movement and its dynamics, explaining that there was hostility between the two liberal faiths. Universalists had separated themselves from traditional Christians who felt entitled to be the sole keeper of faith and morality, while Boston Unitarians considered themselves Christians. Also politically, the newcomers were Jeffersonian anti-Federalists, while Unitarians were confirmed Federalists. Thus the New England elitists rejected Universalism as a creature of Satan. [118]

In the first three decades of the nineteenth century Unitarian congregations were formed in the major cities. Their development was encouraged by a missionary movement financed very meagerly by the American Unitarian Association but enthusiastically supported by Joseph Priestley and students of Henry Ware at Harvard. Ware had been concerned about the need to support existing churches and to spread Unitarianism west. In his 1835 Berry Street lecture he spoke about the need for denominational support:

> I have faith to believe, that if the earnest call of the united ministry were heard, — that if we, brethren, would assume the responsibility of ardently, urgently, solemnly, using our rightful influence, to press this matter upon their conscience, there is a spirit in our congregations to second it with acclamation. When I call to mind what they have done for our Theological School, what they have done for the American Unitarian Association, what for Seamen's Chapel, — objects purely religious, besides their large and frequent secular charities; when I recollect the sacrifices which have been made in Baltimore and many other places; the institution of the "ministry at large" in Boston, and the entire support of a similar ministry by one congregation in New York; when I remember these and other similar facts, I feel assured that our brethren only need to have the real necessity of the case truly laid before them to induce them to do whatever may be necessary on their part to prevent the inroads of irreligion, through the inability of our feebler congregations to support the worship of God. New England never can be without gospel institutions in her poorest villages, if the more favored portions of her children are kept acquainted with their wants.
>
> I have alluded also to the vast regions beyond New England. A great work is to be done there. It will demand the zeal and fidelity … in the older portions of the country to make it certain that that important world in the Western valleys shall be furnished with adequate means of Christian instruction. Our

denomination has its share of that work to perform. We may not dare to withhold ourselves from it. A portion of our means, as many as can be spared of our ministers, must be sent out to help in blessing and training that glorious young giant. Now is the time. Something has already been done. May God bless the beginning, and carry it to its completion! –till, in all the advancing villages of that prosperous domain, the seed of life shall be planted, to grow as they grow, and expand as they extend, and shelter the future millions beneath its capacious shade. Now is the time; –and may the Lord of the harvest send forth laborers unto his harvest.

According to Charles Lyttle, several ministers, among them Ephraim Peabody, James Freeman Clark, William Greenleaf Eliot, George Hosmer and John Pierpoint responded to the call and made their journeys west but not without trepidation. Clark had founded the Louisville church in 1830 and was consulted by prospective ministers as to the challenges facing a new church– could it attract enough members and would they support financially the budding church. [119] Another missionary, Moses G. Thomas, "was dispatched on a five months journey of inquiry to the west." He managed to cover twelve states and found the area ready to support the Christian Unitarianism of Harvard. Pierpoint also had travelled as far west as Saint Louis to preach to a small group of prospective congregants, and he cleared the way for Eliot's ministry covered in chapter three.

The First Independent Church of Baltimore was founded in 1817, and within one year its building was completed, the oldest outside of Boston to be devoted to Unitarianism. Its search for a minister soon led them to Jared Sparks, a Harvard Divinity School graduate who preached his candidate sermon in the fall of 1818. In February 1819 he was hired and on the fifth of May Sparks was ordained with Channing preaching the famous Baltimore sermon that defined Unitarian Christianity. The church continued a ministry of orthodox Unitarianism through the Civil War. Notably, in 1821 Sparks was installed as Chaplain to the House of Representatives. [120]

In 1819 Channing, on his way to Baltimore, visited his sister

Lucy Channing Russell in New York and addressed a small group of religious liberals. On his return he again stopped in New York and spoke in a rented hall. By now the group had grown to several hundred, raised funds, and built the church that was to be All Souls Unitarian Church. In 1821, it called William Ware, a Christian Unitarian, as its first minister. In 1839, Henry Bellows accepted the ministry immediately after graduating from Harvard. He stayed there for forty-three years and became a powerhouse in both Unitarian and national affairs. Bellows accepted the Christian Unitarianism of Channing but also agreed with Parker that some aspects were permanent and some were transient. According to Mark Evens he wrote:

> I am a Christian in faith & theory, an accepter & teacher of historic Christianity; & altho I am free to cancel all the misgrowths & accretions & monstrosities of the Christian Church system-yet beneath all, I feel that the most saving truth[s] have been & continue to be in action. I wish no break of continuity; no rejection or denial of Christian faith & symbols-but only such enlargement of view & purification of feeling-as will enable the world to profit by the more spiritual conception of Christ's teachings, we are able to form & entertain.[121]

Bellows became an active proponent of Unitarianism by lecturing across the young nation to Unitarian groups. In 1861 he formed the New York City Sanitary Commission, designed to help the sick and wounded, particularly those injured during the Civil War. He also travelled to fairs in major cities to exhibit important historical items celebrating the history of New York City. He would later use these to found the institution that became the Metropolitan Museum of Art.

Pittsburgh received a Unitarian church in 1820. In 1825, the American Unitarian Association was formed in Boston to bring a voice to the denomination and act as a clearing house for Unitarian evangelism, albeit with a tiny budget. The year 1827 saw the establishment of a church in Rochester, New York, in 1830 Louisville and Cincinnati followed, and in 1834 the Saint Louis Unitarian Church was founded. All adopted a form of Unitarian

Christianity without the Anglican trappings of King's Chapel. James Freeman Clarke in Louisville defined its theological base in an essay titled "The Five Points of Calvinism and the Five Points of the New Theology." He listed the Calvin doctrines as Absolute Decrees, Atonement by Christ for the Elects, Original Sin, Effectual Calling, and the Perseverance of Saints. Unitarian Christianity was called "The New Theology" or the theology of the future. Its doctrine also had five headings:

> The Fatherhood of God – including holiness, truthfulness and the justice of God, as exemplified by the Sermon on the Mount, glorifying our Father in Heaven.
>
> The Brotherhood of Man – no man is common or unclean, and all have within them the essential goodness of God. Out of this grow all charities, missions, and philanthropies. Jesus was friend of publicans and sinners of the Roman Empire.
>
> The Leadership of Jesus – as a guide in religion and in religious truths. We must learn from Jesus just as the Church did without intercession. All written creeds, such as the Athanasian Creed, are narrow and non-spiritual, and seem to interject the author of the creed as teacher, rather than Jesus.
>
> Salvation by Character – the Kingdom of Heaven is already within us. Salvation is not something outside of us as long as we can find goodness and faith within us. Any outward profession of faith postpones the reward of the inward heaven of Jesus into the future unknown.
>
> Continuance of Human Development in all worlds, and Progress of Mankind onward and upward forever. Man is forever hopeful, forever striving for something better. One can always strive for greater goodness and a fuller life, not as a reward in heaven, but on this earth. It is based on knowledge, not blind acceptance. It sees God in the world around us.[122]

While the Baltimore sermon had defined Christian Unitarianism, some New England ministers were not content with Channing's theology. Emerson and Parker in the 1830s had left the fold, and challenged the denomination to expand its intellectual horizons by relying on intuition and reason. The new faction, if it accepted all or some of the teachings of Christ, rejected the trappings of Christianity and its scripture. It was reluctant to define how Jesus was inspired and rejected the miracles described in the gospels. The more traditional Unitarians called these new thinkers transcendentalists and accused them of infidelity, deism, and pantheism. The result was a split in the denomination.

For thirty years Unitarianism had been in a state of controversy, first with orthodoxy and then with the transcendentalist movement. But the denomination had not expanded intellectually. Octavius Brooks Frothingham, a descendant of Nathaniel Frothingham and minister of Boston's First Church for almost fifty years, characterizes orthodox Unitarian statism with little kindness:

> They had proved, to their own satisfaction at least, that the dogmas of Trinity, Deity of Christ, Vicarious Atonement, Total Depravity and Everlasting Damnation, were unsupported by Scripture and they were in the main content. Precisely what was supported they did not undertake specifically to declare.... The sect as such was torpid. It was respectable and wished to remain so... The Unitarians were about as complacent a set of Christians as ever took ship for the kingdom.[123]

What then, was transcendentalism? It was a movement of nineteenth century writers and philosophers with origins in the works of Europeans such as Emmanuel Kant, Schleiermacher, and DeWitte. In New England its adherents were loosely bound by a system of thought based on the essential unity of all creation, the innate goodness of man, and the supremacy of insight over logic, dogma and experience, the goal of which was the revelation of the deepest truths. Liberal Unitarians, having rejected the despair of Calvinism, now turned to an innate belief in the goodness of humans and rejected the need for divine intercession. In effect it was a manifesto for individual responsibility, and the forerunner of the humanist movement of today. In their religious quest, the transcendentalists discarded the conventions of nineteenth century thought, and what began in dissatisfaction with Unitarianism developed into a repudiation of the whole established Christian Unitarian order. In 1838, Emerson brought the controversy to the Boston public in an address he delivered to the senior class of the Harvard Divinity School. His theme was that man had within him all faculties for a religious and moral life and did not need the biblical stories of Christianity and miracles. He rejected manifold creative power for one will, one mind "in everywhere active, in each ray of the star." It was an unfortunate venue to expose these ideas, the denomination having just passed through a bruising fight with orthodox Calvinists, and provided fodder to those who believed Unitarianism to be a godless heresy bound to damn man to everlasting perdition. Shortly thereafter Emerson resigned from the ministry. In his magazine *The Dial* he continued to acknowledge the power of prayer but with qualifications:

> ... prayers are not made to be overheard, or to be printed, so that we seldom have the prayer otherwise than it can be inferred from the man and his fortunes, which are the answer to the prayer, and always accord with it. Let us not have the prayers of one sect, nor of the Christian Church, but of men in all ages and religions, who have prayed well. The prayer of Jesus is, as it deserves, become a form for the human race... Among the remains of Euripides, we have this prayer; "Thou God of all! infuse light into the souls of men, whereby they may be enabled to know what is the root from whence all their evils spring, and by what means they may avoid them.[124]

Theodore Parker did not go as far as Emerson. While he rejected the concept of a literal interpretation of the Bible and its miracles, he firmly believed in a God that lives deeply in man's soul and generates within him moral virtues of honesty, prudence, and charity. He accepted the efficacy of prayer as a means of composing a person's spirit while at the same time identifying it as a two-way communication with a God who listens to man.[125] Out of this grew his concept of *Absolute Religion*, a belief in God unfettered by unexplainable miracles and contradictions of the Bible. Unlike Emerson, Parker continued to preach, but was rejected by New England conservative Unitarian ministers. He had been installed in the West Roxbury church, but fellow Unitarians refused to exchange pulpits with him. In December 1844, he spoke at the Thursday Lecture of the Ministerial Association. His theme was "The Relation of Jesus to his Age and the Ages," and Octavius Frothingham called his sermon a gorgeous ascription of praise for Jesus. It included, however, a refutation of the literal aspects of the New Testament, and this brought the controversy into the open. One month later, with Parker now barred from Boston churches, a few Unitarian friends decided to give him a pulpit in the Melodion, a Boston assembly hall with enough capacity to serve as a church. By February, Parker was ready to be installed there, having relegated his Roxbury pulpit to a substitute. In preparation for his first service, he asked the Boston Unitarian ministerial organization to answer a set of theological questions regarding the divinity of Jesus, the reality of Bible stories and miracles, and the existence of the devil. He posed twenty-eight questions and then concluded with a challenge:

> I beg you will give your serious attention to the above questions and return me a public answer…as you have publicly placed yourselves in a hostile attitude to me, as some of you have done all in their power to disown me… it is but due to yourselves to open the gospel according to the Boston Association, give the public an opportunity to take the length and breadth of your standard of Unitarian orthodoxy…[126]

There is no record of a formal answer but by January 1846 the Melodion location and Parker's preaching was so successful that he reluctantly severed his association with the Roxbury church. His concept of absolute religion had evolved into a manifestation of man's conscience, guided by a belief in God and the simple teachings of Jesus. It was institutionalized as a distinct departure from Christian Unitarianism and became the historical base of modern liberal theology in many Unitarian churches.

But even as Channing and Parker preached a Unitarian faith, based on Christianity on one side and deist belief in one God on the other, debate would continue within the Unitarian community for the remainder of the century. Was there in their belief system something that could be clearly expressed or distinguished from the orthodox faiths it opposed? Or would Unitarians forever be able to expound fluently on what they did not believe while unable to annunciate what they did believe. This dilemma was frequently the subject of the Berry Street lectures and Unitarian ministers adopted a few simple rules to ensure free and broad discussion of topics at this annual conference. This conference, having met every year save one during the Second World War, is the oldest lecture series on the North American continent (excerpts from many of the lectures are quoted in this work). From its beginning, the conference's purpose was to contribute to the strength of liberal ministries. It is difficult, however, to discern an identifiable Unitarian theology in the lectures. Ministers recognized this and George Washington Burnap stated in his 1850 lecture:

> We must have a theology, — a systematic, positive theology. We want it for ourselves, we want it for those who are without... They demand a theology which shall cover the whole ground, which shall be consistent with itself,... with the Scriptures, and which reason does not reject...

> The generations which established our churches were necessarily acquainted with our theology. They knew its distinctive doctrines; they knew, too, the doctrines to which they were opposed. It was their deliberate preference of the one to the other, which led them to seek a separate organization...

> It is a reproach universally cast upon us, that our faith is a negative one, that our creed consists of articles of unbelief. We ourselves know that this is not true. Christianity is a faith, a belief, not an unbelief. If it is not a faith, something to be believed, it is nothing. We preach, we strive to affect the convictions of

mankind, – of course we preach something that is to be believed. What is that something? I have charity enough to think that the world really wishes to know what that something is.[127]

"That something," was, of course, controversial within the denomination. On the one side were the Christian Unitarians exemplified by Channing and King's Chapel in Boston, with a liturgy that closely resembled Anglican services. All elements of orthodox Christianity were present including references to "Our Lord Jesus Christ" and "the fellowship of the Holy Ghost." It was further exemplified in the Annual Report of the American Unitarian Association (AUA) of 1865:

> "We desire openly to declare our belief as a denomination, so far as it can be officially represented by the American Unitarian Association, that God, moved by his own love, did raise up Jesus to aid in our redemption from sin, did by him pour a fresh flood of purifying life through the withered veins of humanity and along the corrupted channels of the world, and is, by his religion, forever sweeping the nations with regenerating gales from heaven and visiting the hearts of men with celestial solicitations. We receive the teachings of Christ, separated from all foreign admixtures and later accretions, as infallible truth from God."

On the other side were the transcendentalists, who doubted that Christianity was the only true religion and had beliefs that ranged from the acceptance of a supreme being to the search for some form of scientific proof of the deity and faith. Conrad Wright calls them the radicals and points out that they could not abide the declaration of the AUA. As a result, the transcendentalists formed their own Free Religious Association. In between the Christian Unitarians and the transcendentalists was a group that tried to reconcile the two divergent views, but to no avail. Thus Burnap's plea for a Unitarian theology fell on deaf ears. Churches, as they spread across the continent, selected their ministers instead in accordance with the views of the majority of the congregation.

As new churches spread across the East and Midwest, it became increasingly apparent that Harvard Divinity School would be unable to fulfill the demand for ministers. Even though several congregations started with men who had abandoned their Trinitarian roots to become Unitarians, Rockford, Detroit, Erie, and Cleveland were seeking leaders. In response, Harm Jan Huidekoper, a minister in the small Pennsylvania town of Meadville, set out in 1844 to form a Unitarian theological seminary. According to Bumbaugh it was a joint venture between Unitarians and the Christian Connection, a group that was anti-Trinitarian but believed the Bible to be the sole source of authority.[128] A small abandoned church building was purchased, and in October Meadville Theological Seminary opened with five students and four teachers. The seminary taught Unitarian Christianity in the Channing tradition, though the Christian Connection gave it a more orthodox cast than that of Boston churches. Later the school would move to Chicago and become affiliated with Chicago University as the Meadville Lombard School of Theology. In the mean time, with an improved supply of ministers, new churches in the East and Midwest flourished.

In the last half of the nineteenth century, Unitarian ministers had to deal with two major issues. The first was their theology. Would they follow the lead of King's Chapel and Channing and retain the Socinian view of Christ and the Bible, or would they adopt the more modern beliefs of Parker and preach absolute religion? The second was political but with deep moral implications, namely how would they react to slavery and the abolitionists? In the New England environment of relatively wealthy parishioners, some of whom were slave holders, it was easy to avoid the issue, but in the northern states the mood was mixed, and the south was decidedly pro-slavery. As Unitarian churches spread west, most of their ministers actively favored abolition, but this did not necessarily correlate with their theological position.

The First Unitarian Church of Philadelphia was founded by Priestley in 1796 but did not have a full time minister until William Henry Furness arrived in 1825. He was another graduate of Harvard Divinity School and a friend of Emerson. It was thus natural that the theology he preached, Socinian Christianity, had a tinge of transcendentalism. In his fifty year ministry, Furness would begin a trend of social involvement, preaching abolition and tolerance for Jews. Channing had avoided taking a position on abolition, perhaps because he felt it detracted from the emphasis on preaching Christianity. Only towards the end of his ministry did he openly favor it. Theodore Parker, on the other hand, initially was conflicted. As described in his biography, at heart he detested slavery, yet he preached about social classes and at one time asserted that the Anglo Saxon race was superior to Africans. At the same time he advocated the racial integration of Boston schools and churches. By 1853 his abolitionist stance was fully developed, and he denounced the 1846 Mexican War as a brazen attempt to extend slavery. When the Fugitive Slave Act was passed in 1850, Parker called it un-Christian and began a ministry for fugitives. He also chaired the Vigilance Committee in Boston that provided resources to escaped slaves and worked to avoid their capture. [129]

Rochester, New York, received a Unitarian church in 1827 and called Myron Holley as its first minister one year later. He was an early abolitionist, and he even sold his house to provide funds for the movement. Holley remained there for eleven years and preached Socinianism. When he died in 1841 he was eulogized as dying "firmly in the arms of Christian principles and practical good sense." Frederick Holland was appointed in 1842, and while he could be classed as Christian, theologically he shifted the church to Parker's version of transcendentalism. He too was an abolitionist, and in the period before the Civil War, the Rochester church became known for its extremism in fighting against slavery and as a main terminal in the Underground Railroad. Notably, it was also the host for the first women's rights convention, held there in 1848. Thus while the Rochester church generally followed Unitarian conservative theology, it was known for political action and liberal beliefs. It was the first church to accept Darwin's theory of evolution, established a school for immigrant boys, and hosted the Boy Scouts and women's groups.

In 1830, two Unitarian churches were established, one in Cincinnati and the other in Louisville, Kentucky. The Cincinnati church in its early years was split along the theological lines described above. Louisville immediately proceeded to build a church and called as its first minister George Chapman, a Harvard graduate, who only stayed for one year. He was followed by a powerhouse of Unitarian thinking and activism, James Freeman Clarke. According to Gregory McGonigle's biography of Clarke, he graduated from Harvard Divinity School in 1833 and became interested in Goethe's transcendental thinking ultimately using it to shape his preaching.[130] Margaret Fuller, who took over from Emerson as editor of *The Dial*, was his distant cousin, and she also influenced his religious outlook. His personal life was further tied to Unitarianism by marriage to Meadville's Huidekoper's daughter. As McGonigle described his theology:

> Clarke's years of biblical study had brought him to see Jesus as both a conservative and a reformer, not replacing the Law but fulfilling it, and the divinely inspired religion of Jesus not only as compatible with reason but as the very rational foundation of science. To Clarke the life and teachings of Jesus Christ embodied and affirmed what was best in other world religions. Or, to put that differently, Clarke saw his own liberal Christian "intuitions" reflected transcendentally in the religious experiences of the whole human race. In this vein, Clarke remained all his life a transcendalist, but he rejected that label when transcendentalists like his friends Emerson and Parker denied the need for historical precedents, as though they could have the religion of Jesus without Jesus.

Moreover, Clarke foresaw the structure that Unitarians would carry to modernity:

> In accord with the always reforming left-wing of the Protestant tradition, Clarke aimed to gather "a true church of disciples." He formulated three key principles of such a church—the social, the voluntary, and the congregational. Socially, members should

make strong interpersonal connections, and gather not just for worship but in committees and study groups to further the church's purpose. Members should voluntarily regard themselves as equals in the church and voluntarily assume stewardship of the community, supporting it with their financial pledges and offerings. The order of service Clarke developed was ecumenical: he drew on Quaker-inspired silence and meditation, Catholic-inspired holy days, and Methodist-inspired lay singing and preaching. [131]

He remained in Louisville until 1840. During that time he provided guidance and advice to Divinity School graduates who were considering positions in newly organized churches, among them Cincinnati's Ephraim Peabody and Saint Louis candidate William Greenleaf Eliot. In addition, Clarke was the founder of the Unitarian *Western Messenger* magazine as a parallel to Boston's *Christian Examiner* but with a transcendental message.

After leaving Louisville in 1841, Clarke settled in Boston to found the Church of the Disciples, drawing its membership from the greater Boston area. He preached that Jesus was divinely inspired, and insisted that such a belief was compatible with reason. In that church he formed an organization that would later be used by almost all Unitarian congregations, namely a structure of committees and discussion groups. Again citing McGonigle, Clarke expected members to be full partners in church affairs and contribute financially to the upkeep of the church. He established an order of service with responsive readings, hymns and even lay preaching. Even though this caused some resignations, Clarke was one of the very few ministers who exchanged pulpits with Parker after the conservative Unitarian clergy became offended by his rejection of biblical miracles. He was an early advocate of women's suffrage, temperance, and educational reform, and he opposed both the death penalty and slavery. By 1845, the regular attendance for his services was over seven hundred, and in 1849, physically exhausted, he took temporary leave from church leadership. He joined the faculty of Harvard Divinity School in 1867 and continued to write and preach until his death in1888. Clarke's influence in the denomination was enormous. Theologically and organizational he set the tone for Unitarian churches well into the twentieth century.

Chicago was incorporated as a town in 1833. Three years later a small group decided to form a Unitarian church, calling Joseph Harrington as their first minister and raising funds to build a church. For the next fifteen years, the young congregation struggled financially until the arrival of Rush Shippen, a graduate of the newly opened Meadville Seminary who led the congregation for eight years. He was able to put the church on a sound financial footing by transforming the income stream from voluntary contributions to the rental of pews. With the growth of First Church, Shippen was instrumental in founding the Second Unitarian Church in the north side of the city. He later became secretary of the American Unitarian Association.

One of the most active abolitionist ministers was Samuel Joseph May. His influence seems to be underrated in Unitarian history. In 1822 he accepted the ministry in a small Congregational church in Brooklyn, Connecticut, and adopted an Arian version of Unitarianism that resulted in an exodus of Trinitarians. His theology was somewhat mixed. He professed to be a Unitarian Christian, but he favored communion for all and administered immersion baptism. It was in effect a mixture of orthodox Christianity, Arianism and Universalism. His position was clearly expressed in his 1853 Berry Street essay on reform. In addition to preaching abolition, he invited African-Americans to participate in worship services. He also called for social action to curb the evils of love of money and wealth creation, and he wanted state laws to regulate them. He thus paralleled the socialist views of England's Henry Solly. He quickly became a pacifist and even criticized the founding fathers for entering into the Revolutionary War. Considering drink evil, he organized a temperance society. None of this made him popular with the citizens of the small Connecticut town. In 1827 he worked to reform the state's school system, a path that would be followed by William Greenleaf Eliot in Saint Louis. By1830 abolitionist activities dominated his ministry and he formed the New England Anti-Slavery Society. In 1845 he became minister to the Church of the Messiah in Syracuse and stayed there until 1867. While an ardent abolitionist, he also espoused equal rights for women and formed a small union for needle women.[132] But his main cause until the Civil War was opposition to slavery. As he stated in his Berry Street lecture:

> I know very well there are some ministers and moralists who incline to regard "the love of money" with the institutions and devices of men for the acquisition and perpetuation of property... [and] for a long while regarded Slavery, *i.e., as an organic sin*; ...a sin so inwrought into the very constitution of society, that the attempt by man to eradicate it would be vain, and the condemnation of the individuals who were involved in the mysteries of its iniquity was uncharitable and cruel. And yet we see with our own eyes that that strong condemnation of our national sin... has at length effectually aroused the people of the non-slaveholding States to see and feel the tremendous wickedness of Slavery—the individual, domestic, social wrongs and vices which are inseparable from it—the perhaps irreparable damage which it has done to our Republic.[133]

At the crossroads of slavery and abolition was the District of Columbia. Slavery was legal in Washington. The Unitarian Society of Georgetown, established in 1815, and, by 1821, had evolved into the First Unitarian Church of Washington. Among its founders were President John Quincy Adams and his vice president John C. Calhoun. The church was actively abolitionist, and in 1824 its minister Robert Little preached anti-slavery sermons. This was continued by William Henry Channing, whom the Church history calls a vigorous opponent of slavery and advocate of equal rights for women. The church theology was Unitarian Christian in nature, paralleling that of most Unitarian churches .

The existence of Unitarian churches in the south was, in general, an issue often ignored in the north. According to Clement Eaton, there were several Unitarian churches in the south, and their ministers and congregations were deeply offended by Unitarian activities to free slaves. One church in particular was in Charleston,

South Carolina. Its first minister was Anthony Forster who was married to a daughter of Priestley. He had read Priestley's works and became a Unitarian.[134] In 1819, the Second Independent Church of Charleston called as their minister Harvard graduate Samuel Gilman. Gilman was an Arminian and Socinian, but at times he deviated from Unitarian Christianity, feeling that its orthodoxy was extreme. By 1834, the congregation was calling itself the Archdale Unitarian Church. Gilmore's ministry was highly successful and in 1852 the membership numbered four hundred. Gilmore, however, owned house slaves, and he tried to take a middle path by avoiding any mention of slavery in his sermons and writings.[135] His wife, Caroline Howard Gilmore, a prolific writer, was not so diplomatic, and she staunchly defended the institution of slavery and the southern way of life. She and her husband conformed to local custom, and the couple quickly became central figures in the city's social and literary life.[136]

Another southern Unitarian minister was Theodore Clapp. Clement Eaton calls him the most independent minister of the Old South, who, despite his liberalism, justified slavery. A native of Massachusetts, he was a graduate of Yale and of Andover Theological Seminary, where he received a traditional Calvinist education. In 1822, he was appointed minister of the New Orleans Presbyterian Church but abandoned it two years later after being bitterly attacked for his unorthodox beliefs. Clapp then set up an independent church which became exceedingly popular and was attended by many prominent people. With religious views quite similar to Unitarian doctrine, he became an advocate of tolerance toward all classes: Catholics, atheists, and skeptics.[137] He too was an ardent defender of slavery, going so far as to find biblical justification for the practice. His journey towards liberal religion began when he rejected Calvinistic doctrines of sin and predestination and began to preach a version of Universalism deemed heretical by the Mississippi Presbytery. Expelled by the Presbytery in 1832, most of Clapp's congregation supported him, and in 1833 the church was renamed the First Congregational Society and joined the American Unitarian Association four years later. With a great interest in anatomy, Clapp was appointed to the board of what would become the Tulane Medical School. For a time, medical school classes were even taught in the church building, and the first commencement was held there.

In Unitarian histories, the Pacific Coast has generally been neglected, but the San Francisco Unitarian Universalist Church is of particular importance in the denomination. It was founded in 1850 through the efforts of Captain Frederick William Macondray, a famous sea captain and China trader, and became known as a Unitarian outpost in a rough and tumble west.[138] In 1860, Thomas Starr King began his ministry there. He was brought up as a Universalist but had been pastor of the Hollis Street Unitarian Church in Boston for eleven years and was noted as a gifted speaker and inspiring leader. After eleven years he left New England for the west. According to his biographers Celeste DeRoche and Peter Hughes he described Christianity "not as a creed or an institution, but as a spirit, a secret agency or force underlying the religious experience. He thought that God's spirit was to be found both inside and outside the church, in works of secular art and in private lives, and found more unity and truth in shared public expression than in the speculation of dogma and theology."[139] King became very active in California politics, touring the west with a pro-Union message and in all likelihood preserving the state for the Union. Compared to the teachings of eastern Harvard graduates and Meadville students, King's theology was more liberal than transcendentalism and far removed from Unitarian Christianity. He made his mark as a patriot and an ardent opponent of secession. Starting in 1861, King traveled across California urging people to support the Union and bring an end to slavery. He raised money for the Western Sanitary Commission that cared for Union troops hurt during the Civil War, and he draped the San Francisco church pulpit with the stars and stripes to demonstrate his love for the country. When he died in 1864 at the age of thirty-nine he had preached only seven sermons, yet the whole city mourned his passing and a salute was fired from Alcatraz.

Horatio Stebbins had the unenviable task of following King. He was minister from 1864 to 1900, a period that was marked by church growth and a move to its present site. His theology was a modified Unitarian Christianity, summarized by the church history as "promoting charity and good works, and to strengthen and increase the life of the mind and heart and spirit that is under God and Christ." During his ministry many illustrious Unitarian and civic leaders came west to speak at the church, among them Ralph Waldo Emerson, Andrew Peabody, Julia Ward Howe, Susan B. Anthony, and Booker T. Washington. After leaving the ministry Stebbins became president of the College of California, later to become the University of California.

Stebbins was followed by Bradford Leavitt who led the church until 1913 and thus had to carry it through the famous and disastrous earthquake of 1906. Miraculously, the church building survived, but the damage disrupted services for some time. Homes of church members were also destroyed, and many left the city. Following the Unitarian tradition of involvement in civic affairs Leavitt worked on a relief commission closely aligned with the city administration. He later exposed corruption in City Hall, resulting in the Mayor's conviction and the resignation of the entire Board of Supervisors. Regarding theology he opined: "The struggles of the coming century will be largely social – personal salvation will give way to social salvation." The Christian Registry, however, was very pessimistic about the future of the West Coast for Unitarianism. Prior to the 1906 earthquake, Leavitt refuted this view. He said: "Never in the history of this coast has our situation been as promising as it is today...church debts have been reduced, six new churches have been organized...two new buildings have been erected that are free from debt...and a new divinity school [Starr King School for the Ministry] with a house and lot presented to the school."

By 1860, most southern Unitarian churches had disappeared or were in decline because of the anti-slavery stance of the denomination. In Augusta, Georgia, Mobile, Alabama, Nashville, and Wheeling churches closed, and Washington and Baltimore congregations split into those that wanted to retain slavery and those that favored abolition.[140] At this point all northern Unitarian churches were openly anti-slavery, and with the outbreak of the Civil War, all drew together to support abolition and applauded President Lincoln's Emancipation Proclamation. In Chicago and Saint

Louis, Unitarian ministers formed sanitary commissions to provide medical services to the northern army and a cleaner environment for the poor. Like their English brethren, they worked for universal suffrage and campaigned to provide better working conditions in factories and reduced working hours. The denomination provided chaplains to the army, and fully supported the war. Theologically, in many churches there was a contest between faith and reason. In 1897 Charles Carlson Everett addressed this topic in his Berry Street lecture:

> Men have brought many precious offerings to God, but none more precious than the sacrifice of their reason at what was called his shrine. I do not mean, of course, that Christian worship was at any time the worship merely of unreason; but so far as the thought of God came into direct conflict with human reason, so far it obviously represented unreason, enthroned and deified... We see that when the nature of both is understood there is and can be no strife between them. We do not find reason everywhere manifested in the world. There is much that appears irrational. Faith, so far as it is complete, affirms the absolute rationality of the universe. Where it cannot see, it believes. It postulates whatever seems to it absolutely needed, in order to represent to itself this rationality... This has created ideals rising far above whatever the outward world can furnish. If anything could be the type of the power that is working in and through all things, surely it is this...If we take our place, as each one should among those who are striving to bring about a purer thought and a larger life, our only ground of hope for a final victory is faith in the essential reasonableness of man, the essential rationality of the world and in the supreme Reason that rules the universe.[141]

These were prophetic words, because they presaged the turning of Unitarian Churches to Humanism. Curtis W. Reese had challenged the denomination to abandon its Christian and theist-based belief system when he was minister of the church in Des Moines, Iowa from 1915 to 1919. At the beginning of his tenure he was convinced that Unitarianism was based on the idea of God the universal father, the brotherhood of man, and the right to freedom of belief. By 1917, Reese moved to embrace a more humanist view of religion and incorporated his new philosophy in sermons and in an address at the Harvard Divinity School three years later. While Reese's work was influential, the flagship humanist church in the denomination at this time was in Minneapolis. Founded in 1881, its first article of incorporation reads: "Where people without regards to their theological differences may unite for mutual helpfulness in the intellectual, moral and religious culture and humane work." The church's fourth minister, John Hassler Dietrich, served the church for twenty-two years and established in 1916 the defining humanist characteristics that still prevail. One year later he fashioned what became known as the fundamental tenets of Humanism:[142]

> The conviction that man as the highest product of the creative process, with nothing above or beyond him but his own ideals as an end in himself and not the purposes of a superior being.
>
> Faith in the possibility of improving human life.
>
> Belief in the essential unity of mankind and the necessity of bringing man to a consciousness of this unity.
>
> Faith in man–belief that the power to realize this is great.

With Dietrich and Reese in attendance, these tenets were challenged at the 1917 Western Unitarian Conference by ministers of the two Saint Louis Unitarian Churches, William Laurence Sullivan of the Church of the Messiah, and George Rowland Dodson of the Church of the Unity.[143] Precisely because of the humanist cast of its ministry, however, the Minneapolis church thrived. Dietrich was active throughout the Midwest, spreading the humanist philosophy with lectures and weekly radio broadcasts. His hour-long sermons became famous in Minnesota, and the church grew, with attendance at times reaching one thousand. Dietrich felt that the expressed freedom of belief of the denomination allowed for Humanism. The enabling characteristics of Unitarianism, he asserted, were a revolt against orthodox Christianity and an insistence on intellectual integrity.[144] By the 1950s, roughly twenty percent of Unitarian churches were humanist.

In 1900 the American Unitarian Association decided that it could no longer ignore liberal religions in other countries. The organization formed the *International Council of Unitarians and Other Liberal religious Thinkers and Workers*. In 1907, it felt ready to bring together all who qualified under that title. Accordingly, in September of that year, more than nineteen hundred Unitarians from all over the world assembled in Boston for the International Congress of Unitarians. There were 2,300 registered delegates "representing four of the great world religions,"[145] presumably Christianity, Judaism, Buddhist and Hindu. In addition, many more faith groups participated, including Muslims and Roman Catholics. International delegates also attended, including more than a hundred from England. William Greenleaf Eliot commented on their conclusions: "The religion of Jesus is superior to dogma and authority. Freedom is as good for religion as is government." He added that there was a great manifestation of powers working for the good of man, and thus also for the kingdom of God.[146]

American Unitarian ministers might worry that their theology was not strong but in the last decades of the nineteenth century this did not prevent them from vigorously espousing many social issues. They abhorred slavery, deplored the slaughter of thousands during the Civil War, advocated women's rights, and fought for improvement of the working classes. Throughout the struggle for a theology continued, submerged, perhaps, in the desire by Unitarians to deal with the secular world that they knew rather than with the controversial spiritual world. Thus, doubts arose about the very existence of God. Who was this God that allowed destructive wars and indiscriminate slaughter and destruction? When both sides of a mortal conflict asserted that God was on their side who could claim victory? Liberal religion, not bound by rigid dogma or in a belief in a God who supervised man's action, was found wanting.

At the same time, rapid scientific advancements eclipsed the belief in divine supervision of the world. Darwin propounded the theory of evolution. The telegraph revolutionized communications and Western Union was founded. Edison invented the telephone, the incandescent light bulb, and recording of sound and music. Radio established a new medium for communication. Automobiles came into being, and the world was traversed and united by railroads. The first airplanes appeared. It was science and technology that defined the world and God was not necessary for such a definition. As the 1860s began, Unitarian ministers struggled between the need to reconcile faith and science. Charles Carroll Everett recognized this in his 1868 Berry Street lecture titled *The Faith of Science and the Science of Faith*:

> The words *faith* and *science* are often used as if they stood to one another in a relation not merely of antithesis, but in one of opposition and exclusion. We often speak of the realm of faith and the realm of science, as if each was a world by itself. As soon as an object enters the realm of science, we are apt to feel that it has left the realm of faith; and so long as an object remains in the realm of faith, it is felt to be, by that fact, excluded from the realm of science. Many believe that the realm of science is surely and steadily encroaching upon that of faith; and many are looking, some with dread and some with hope, to see the realm of faith becoming smaller and smaller, until at last there will be no place left for it, and science shall reign supreme and alone. Indeed, this antagonism between faith and science is felt by many to constitute the great dramatic or even tragic interest of the present age. This whole view, however, is founded upon error. There is no such thing as a realm of science apart from the realm of faith. They represent simply different sides of the same knowledge. Faith, we may say, furnishes the basis, and science the superstructure; or we may say, furnishes the material, and science elaborates this

material into its perfect form. Faith, we may say, is the nebula, and science the completed world which is developed out of it... Thus there is no science that does not imply a corresponding faith, and there is no faith that is not capable of a scientific elaboration. The only difference between what we call the realm of science and what we call the realm of faith is, that the realm of faith is the broadest, for the reason that the whole extent of it has not yet been developed into science... The progress of science neither encroaches upon nor limits faith. It simply elaborates more and more of the material of faith into its fitting and true form. But the material is still as truly that of faith, as it was in its simplest and most unformed state.

What, then, is the basis of our faith in the inductions of science? It is interesting to see how loath the human mind is to give up belief in outward foundations and supports, and the naïve confidence with which it assumes them. Nothing is more natural than the Hindoo theory, that the earth rests upon an elephant, and the elephant upon a tortoise; or than that of the old lady who believed that the earth rested upon a rock, and that upon another, and that there were rocks all the way down. The mind naturally assumes a foundation, and it is long before the question forces itself, "Upon what does this foundation rest?" so it lays rocks beneath the earth, or places a patient elephant beneath it; it forms crystal spheres to support the stars, and thinks that all is firmly based. We can now hardly realize the importance of the revolution by which the mind reaches the conviction, that there is no outward support for anything; that there is no point of rest in all the material universe; that everything floats, if that can be said to float that is not even upheld by any medium; that sun and moon and stars, and the earth itself, move through the infinite space upheld by nothing; that there is no arch for the stars, no pillars for the earth; that there is only vacancy above and below everything.

A revolution similar to this has yet to be accomplished in the world of mind and the spirit. We return to the question: On what rests our faith in the inductions of science? John Stuart Mill affirms, with naïve simplicity like that of the old lady who thought that there were rocks all the way down, that faith in induction rests upon induction; in other words, that there is induction all the way down. And there is nothing that shows how natural it is for men to assume foundations without asking what they rest upon, than the fact that so many accept this statement as all-sufficient; that so many, in fact, cannot be made to see why the statement, that faith in induction rests upon induction, does not explain every thing completely. We thus see the possibility of the science of religious faith, and also what must be the nature of this science. As physical science forms itself about faith in the absolute order, so religious science gathers about faith in the absolute goodness.

He did resolve, as did many other Unitarian ministers, that a free and liberal religion such as Unitarianism was able to reconcile science with faith, and, perhaps more than any other faith based movement, was able to establish a rational belief system. Yet in this changing environment, traditional Unitarian church membership did not grow commensurate with population growth. Perhaps it was simpler and more appealing for the general population to believe in Jesus as a savior who died for man's sins than to search for a life force that was hard to define. Perhaps science was more powerful than religion, Whatever the reason, Unitarian ministers struggled with this problem , and in 1919 Richard Boynton made an observation still true today:

> Unitarianism, at least in the United States…has been from the beginning, and is still without notable exceptions, the religion of a ruling caste. Dr. Oliver

Wendell Holmes characterized them aptly as "the
Brahmin caste of New England." The point scarcely
requires argument... Nor is the phenomenon one of
Boston or New England merely. You find much the
same type of people in all our churches, wherever
you go. With scarcely an important exception, our
principal church buildings are found only in the most
prosperous and beautiful residential sections of the
communities in which they stand... Unquestionably,
to my mind, it accounts in a considerable part for
the painful slowness of our growth as a religious
body. There are not enough of this kind of people
in any community, to whom we can appeal, to make
many more Unitarians of the possessing and satisfied
classes, and their satellites, than we now have.[147]

Part of the problem not addressed by Boynton was the difficulty
of fashioning programs and services for people outside of his
description. The American Unitarian Association had limited funds
for evangelization, and few ministers were good at it. Boynton
made his observation at the end of the Civil War and described a
denomination rent by both the conflict as well as by social actions not
always accepted by the general public. The abolitionist movement,
often spearheaded by Unitarian churches, was a precursor of social
action that permeated Unitarian theology for the first decades of
the twentieth century. The Civil War, while it ended slavery, had not
brought equality to the nation. African Americans were not always
accepted in traditional Christian churches, and some elements of
the white community insisted on segregated facilities from water
fountains to railroad cars. Most Unitarian churches, by contrast, had
been integrated before the Civil War. Unitarian women also took the
lead in the suffragette movement. Notably, Susan B. Anthony led
the drive for women's rights to property, inheritance, and ultimately
the vote, the last granted only in 1920, after her death. With the
outbreak of World War I, many Unitarian churches also actively
opposed American participation and sermonized against the war.

During the nineteenth century, Unitarian thought came of age.
Starting with Channing, it developed the multifaceted theology

that is still used today. More ministers during that time quoted Parker than Channing, and, one might argue that the concept of splitting the permanent from the transient had become an enduring characteristic of the Unitarian movement. Its further evolution into the modern Unitarian world is described in the following chapters.

CHAPTER 3.

A River Runs Through It.

In the 1830s three Midwest river cities became targets of Unitarian missionaries. Churches were started in Louisville and Cincinnati by Moses Thomas and five years later a church was established in Saint Louis. Cincinnati and Saint Louis in particular were growing rapidly as a result of river traffic, had large German and Catholic populations, and contained small but growing communities of businessmen that rejected Calvinist doctrine. Despite the fact that Ohio and Missouri were free states, the question of slavery was divisive for all three cities because of their commercial and business ties to the South. The First Congregational [Unitarian] church in Cincinnati started with a theology similar to that of the Saint Louis church – Christian Unitarian – and both later split on doctrinal grounds, only to be reconciled and reunited as transcendentalism took hold. There was, however, a major difference between them: in Cincinnati the splinter group was ultra-Unitarian Christian, while in Saint Louis the seceding members formed a more liberal transcendental church. The conservatives ultimately rejoined the main church in Cincinnati. In Saint Louis, the Unitarian Christian parent Church of the Messiah was absorbed in the off-shoot transcendental Church of the Unity. During the nineteenth century both churches had ministers deeply involved in civic affairs and were prominent in furthering the growth of their cities. Their pastors would play a major role in the development of higher education, Vickers with the University of Cincinnati and Eliot with Washington University in Saint Louis.

UNITARIANISM IN CINCINNATI

Cincinnati's first Unitarian Church was established in 1830. From the start, Cincinnati's population was more liberal than that of Saint Louis. Its German population took root after the Revolutionary War when Hessian troops elected to stay in the newly formed United States. In 1814 they formed Saint John's German Protestant Church, and it was not until the twentieth century that the church developed Unitarian views, joining the American Unitarian Association in 1924. Germans who fled the 1848 revolution also found a home in the city, and noted abolitionists Henry Ward Beecher and Levi Coffin settled there and made the city a waypoint on the underground railway. Close by in Yellow Springs was Antioch College. Its president, Horace Mann, was a transplanted Boston Unitarian, an ardent proponent of public school education as well as a former member of the United States congress. An abolitionist, he often preached at First Church.

As with most Unitarian churches of that era, Cincinnati called its first ministers from the pool of graduates of Harvard Divinity School. From the start, there was tension between the more liberal ministers and the conservative congregation. According to Charles Lyttle, early church members subscribed to a covenant of "communicants to the Lord's Supper" that affirmed the belief in "Jesus Christ the Son of God, exalted to be Prince and Savior," a more orthodox throwback to Channing's Unitarian Christianity and more akin to the tenets of the late sixteenth century Socianian Racovian Catechism . Named the First Congregational Church of Cincinnati, E. B. Hall was its first minister, but he lasted only eight months.[148] He was followed by Ephraim Peabody, who stayed four years, after which the position was filled by a number of visitors and candidates. By the late 1830s, William Greenleaf Eliot of Saint Louis and Freeman Clark of Louisville, managed to persuade William Henry Channing to come to Cincinnati, but he too ran afoul of the members, espousing abolition at a time when Cincinnati was vigorously debating the issue. He left in 1840 and was replaced by James Perkins, as *Minister to the Poor*, a layman, former farmer, and later a lawyer, who was appointed as full minister and remained with the church until his death in 1849. His orthodoxy would eventually cause a rift in the church. His view of the Last Supper is exemplified in an article for the Western Messenger of July 1849:

> Jesus, as we have heard from both Luke and Paul, said "do this in remembrance of me."Are not those words clear? Can theological acuteness twist them from the obvious meaning?...And while the misery of knowing and feeling what he could not make others know and feel weighed upon his spirit ; he tells them that his end is nigh, that he is about to die a Passover for them, to save them from a worse fate than befell the Egyptians, and asks them, henceforth when he is gone to eat a new Passover in remembrance of him, as heretofore they had eaten in remembrance of God's care over their fathers...I should then receive the Lord's Supper as an Ordinance; as a rite established to communicate our Savior, and to knit bands of brotherhood between those whom fortune separates; and the obligation to attend that Rite, I conceive, could not be stronger than it is.

This view of Christianity was certainly atypical of prevailing Unitarian beliefs of that time, though Lyttle himself felt that he left a "strong and united church" to his successor Abiel Livermore.[149] Livermore also was a graduate of Harvard Divinity School, and he served the Unitarian church in Keene, New Hampshire before coming to Cincinnati in 1850. During his time in New Hampshire, he was undoubtedly exposed to the transcendentalism of Emerson and Parker. Livermore realized, as had Channing, that Unitarian Christianity could not exist without the application of reason to the scriptures, and he explained his view in his essay on Reason and Revelation:

> Man is gifted with a faculty or capacity variously called in common parlance, reason, mind, common sense, understanding, – that searches, apprehends and judges concerning all that falls within its cognizance. By this power …he is able to discriminate between truth and error upon all subjects whatever. By this he generalizes principles from facts and predicts facts from principles. Into this crucible he throws arts, sciences philosophies, religions and the dross and gold are divided…For by it he determines the meaning even of Scripture itself, decides therefore what to believe, what do, whom worship, and which of the numerous and increasing theories of Christianity he shall adopt as his own.[150]

Livermore stayed with the church until 1856 and was able to moderate the strident Christian nature of its service format, and managed to reconcile a church torn between Bostonian conservatism and Parker's Absolute Religion. The controversy within the church was rekindled, however, after it called Moncure D. Conway as its next minister. This was the pre-Civil War period, and while Eliot in Saint Louis deplored slavery without dwelling on the topic, Conway was a staunch abolitionist. He had been minister in the Unitarian church of Washington, D.C., but in his words: "I was by a majority of five declared to be too radical in my discourse on slavery for the critical condition of that latitude…" Conway was no more mellow when he arrived in Cincinnati and defiantly celebrated his view on Christianity in his discourse and sermon titled *East and West,* preached on May 1, 1850. Asserting first that he was not clerical, he then added that he did not believe in Christianity. Nature was not deemed to be so imperfect as to create a devil that could outwit the rest of the world. Conway stated that he could not believe that Jesus was born without a human father, and enumerated the biblical miracles that stretched nature and credulity, dispensing with whatever vestige of conservative preaching that might have appealed to the congregation. This was his message:

> It is the East that has a pervasive darkness that brought us the Gods and Goddesses of mythology, Jehovah

and "his thunderbolts of Hebrew Mythology" and bloody sacrifices in the name of religion. On the other hand there is the West that brought Christianity to the world and with it new theories concerning God and the soul. We do not doubt that the old legends, which we are called on to substitute for all that is vital in Christianity, the old creeds about the Trinity and Vicarious Atonement, the miracles, etc., were all appropriate institutions in their time; they were legitimized by the Oriental fancy, in the world's night or twilight; but our lot is not appointed in Asia Minor, nor is our lot to bask in the sun like dervishes. Our work is to live true lives and make pure homes in Cincinnati and to help make America a free and happy land.[151]

Implied in his lengthy sermon was that those with conservative Unitarian Christian views who supported the Cincinnati Lord's Supper were outmoded and no longer in touch with reality. Having offended some fifty of the wealthier parishioners, Conway watched as they left to form the Church of the Redeemer. In turn, Conway would remain pastor of the First Congregational Church until 1862.

Having broken with the First Congregational Church, the Church of the Redeemer was served by visiting ministers and laymen until the arrival of Amory Dwight Mayo in 1863. Mayo preached his first sermon on February 1. It was titled *A Christian Church* and, judging by its tenor, nowhere else in the denomination was there a more fervent Christian. The only time he mentioned the word *Unitarian* was in the second paragraph of a very lengthy treatise, and it was quickly dismissed by the phrase: "We are called a Unitarian Church by the people; we have named ourselves *The Church of the Redeemer*. We accept both these honored names; but both these, and all other good names, are only our way of saying that we claim to be a Christian church according to our highest conception of the religion of Jesus Christ." As he continued, he explained that this required a literal interpretation of the Bible:

We use the Bible as the record of God's highest revelation to Mankind. We do not set it up as our idol to worship, or read its paragraphs as theological charms to conjure with, or compromise its value as impossible fancy of verbal inspiration. But in the Hebrew nation and its greatest men we see the highest religious inspiration vouchsafed to any ancient people; and in Jesus and the early history of Christianity, the appearance of the absolute religion of love…But the New Testament is the Christian's Bible and there is enough to save us and all the world from superstition and sin.[152]

He went on to explain the doctrine that governs Christian life and asked those that did not believe to join in learning about Jesus:

We invite all to come and help us learn of Christ, confident that those will remain with whom we can have a practical sympathy in faith or that union of charity which is better than unanimity of belief. We shall freely expose all religious doctrines that seem to us untrue. But we assail no man's religious character because of an honest faith, and rejoice that men and churches can do so much for religion, in spite of their error.

The implication was that Mayo's Christian faith was the one true religion as defined by his very orthodox Christianity without any expression of Unitarian beliefs or call for human reason. This was much more conservative than Channing's Christian Unitarianism and more rigid than the belief of most confirmed Arians. The address was given in the middle of the Civil War, but Mayo makes only one reference to the conflict: "We see in the present condition of our beloved country the most painful proof of their [Christ and Scriptures] absence in the past; and we have no confidence that America can be a true Republic, until Americans are converted to Christ's religion of love." It is hard to find in Unitarian literature another overt call for conversion to Christianity.

Meanwhile, by 1867 the war had ended, and Thomas Vickers took over the leadership of First Church. He continued the Cincinnati tradition of Unitarian involvement in the life of the city and the alliance with liberal Judaism. Vickers became deeply immersed in civic affairs and made no secret of his views on religion and how it might interact with public policy. He spoke at liberal Protestant churches regardless of their denomination, among them St. John's German Protestant Church before it turned to Unitarianism. His address to the group was part of the celebration of the laying of the corner stone of that church. It was an affirmation of free thought and reason. He called it:

> ...a solemn and inspiring occasion... for the purpose of celebrating one of the most solemn acts of worship in which the modern world can participate – in order, in the name of both God and Man, for the spiritual advantage and improvement of the community in which we live, as a representative and illustration of the indissoluble union between the temporal and the eternal, between heaven and earth, between Deity and humanity, to lay the foundation stone of a new temple of religion.[153]

He went on to attack traditional Christianity as destroying the spiritual essence of religion and asserted that the modern Church must become a sanctuary for free thought. One week later, Archbishop J. B. Purcell took the occasion of the laying of a cornerstone for the Rose Catholic Church to attack Vickers as having reviled Catholicism and claimed that it no longer allowed free thought or allowed men the freedom to err without Church punishment: "Arius, Macedonius, Pelegaius, Manes, Origen, Luther, Calvin, Zwinglius...and all the heresiachs who fell like withered branches from the tree of life were not led by her to the stake." He conveniently neglected to mention that Catholic heretics during the inquisition were prosecuted by the Church but then were turned over to civil authorities for execution. Why then this vehement attack? A new controversy had engulfed Cincinnati in 1867, eventually involving not only the two ministers of the Unitarian churches but also Archbishop Purcell. It was called the Cincinnati Bible War, and it began when Catholic members of the public school board attempted to bring parochial schools under their control and treat them like public schools. Parochial school teachers would become school employees, and Catholic school buildings would be purchased by the city and administered by the board. Under the regulations, Catholic schools would adopt the textbooks used by public schools and there would be no religious instruction during normal school hours, however, the schools would be open weekends for such instruction. Cincinnati public schools had a long tradition of daily Bible reading and hymn singing to open the school day. In composition the school board matched the religious make-up of the city, with Catholic, Protestant and Jewish members joining a few non-sectarians. The board also included the two Unitarian ministers, Vickers and Mayo, but on opposing sides. To settle the controversy, an amendment to the resolution of school consolidation was offered and accepted that forbade all Bible reading and hymn singing in schools.

Predictably Vickers opposed Bible reading in public schools on the grounds that children came from diverse religions and national origin, and should not be exposed just to Christianity. He also argued that the framers of the constitution, specifically Jefferson and Madison, had established the United States as a secular nation, and therefore no public institution was allowed to favor one religion over another. With Vickers view of the Bible as just another religious text and not revealed in any sense, his position matched that of the majority of Unitarian ministers of that time, with the exception perhaps of the strictest Unitarian Christians. Mayo was equally vocal in advocating Bible reading and, with some hyperbole, considered the book to be "the simplest, strongest, and a universally acknowledged statement of this absolute religion of love to God and man, which has been the ideal of every modern state, and the creative principle of modern civilization. When a child reads the Ten Commandments and the Sermon on the Mount, repeats the Lord's Prayer and beholds the character of Jesus, he does not need to be told; there is religion and morality in the fountain head."[154] He then went on to blast Vickers, and with him Unitarianism as a whole:

> Suppose when the Rev. Mr. Vickers entered his new church on Plum Street (which is probably after his

confession of faith, not to be dedicated to that weak decoction of religion called Unitarianism) suppose his trustees should offer him, as the decision of the congregation, a resolution saying that 'that religious instruction, reading of religious books including the Holy Bible and singing of religious hymns were forbidden within its walls it strikes me that the reverend gentleman would conclude that his occupation as teacher of religion in that house was gone.

Mayo was railing against Catholics and atheist, lumping Vickers among the latter, because both groups opposed the consolidation of schools and Bible reading. The Catholics did not want to expose their children to the St. James version of the Bible but welcomed the tax relief of the consolidation. The atheists, with whom Mayo included many Protestants and Jews, did not want their children exposed to any religion outside of the home and church. Mayo also brushed aside the argument that under the United States Constitution no tax support should be granted to any religion, and schools that required Bible reading fell under that prohibition. In fact, with great prescience, he argued:

To what does this whole style of reasoning conduct us? If correct one Catholic citizen of the United States, or any State, may demand that all recognition of religion shall be put out of public affairs because there is no other religion that than the Catholic, which the State will not adopt. One atheistic father may demand that all acknowledgment of God shall be put out of our common schools because it is an offense to his conscience to pay a tax to a government that acknowledges the truth of religion.

In the end, the school consolidation never took place. Mayo left the Church of the Redeemer in 1872, and Vickers left the ministry in 1874 to become chief librarian of the Cincinnati Public Library and subsequently rector of the University of Cincinnati. In November 1875 the two Unitarian churches decided that neither was doing well in membership or finances, and they were reunited under the old name, First Congregational Church. In 1876 it called Charles Wendte as its minister and by 1877 modified its name to the First Congregational Unitarian Church.

Wendte had preached several times at the Church of the Redeemer before the reunification, and he was acceptable to its conservative Christian Unitarians. What was surprising was that the more liberal members who remained in the Congregational Church would allow his definition of Unitarianism. Wendte tried to make clear how he defined his faith in a treatise published in 1877 titled *What do Unitarians Believe?*[155] He began by paying homage to the non-creedal nature of the movement and its diversity of beliefs but in its opening paragraphs he identified his innate belief that Unitarians are part of Christianity: "This is the natural and logical result of that free and fearless use of the reason in religious questions which distinguishes Unitarians above all other Christians." He then continued: "...we believe in Christianity as the purest and best form of religion." Yet he rejected the Christianity of Luther, Calvin and even Channing, while claiming: "We are constantly receiving new revelations of divine wisdom from the Holy Spirit of God, which as Jesus himself said, was to continue his work and to lead us into all truth." At this point one can only surmise that Channing's view of Unitarianism was more liberal than that of Wendte, who seemed to embrace a theology much like that of Boston's King's Chapel. Wendte then turned to the Unitarian definition of God and postulated that it included a belief in his perfect nature, then listed the characteristics of God that Unitarians did not believe in. In the end he asserted that God is infinite and beyond the understanding of man. Revelation and the Bible were treated the same way. Wendte exhorted his congregation to believe in both and then immediately defined what it should not believe. Thus the congregation was asked to revere the Bible as superior to other sacred religious texts such as the vedas and the Koran: "It is the book of books to us...our manual of devotion, our treasury of religious instruction, our unfailing source of spiritual nourishment." His definition of Christ was based on the gospels but without the miracles and deeds of the Bible and he did not identify Christ as a mediator between man and God. He then modified this and stated that Jesus' mediation was not official but purely moral and that Christ remained an example "that we should follow in his steps." Wendte remained with the First Church until 1882. He was followed by George A. Thayer who served the church until 1916.

Thayer's tenure marked a transition for the First Church, and his1906 sermon on *What Do Unitarians Believe* may well be one of the best expressions of early twentieth century Unitarian theology. In straight-forward language he described the belief system still prevalent in the majority of Unitarian theist congregations. Briefly touching on the non-creedal nature of churches, he stressed their independence and freedom from the hierarchical structures of other Protestant and Catholic denominations. Thayer postulated that Unitarianism, like other religions, had to be modernized and adjusted to the advances in science, knowledge, and history. He described the new Unitarian as a man of the twentieth century:

> The new Unitarian, because of his exemption from any standard of authority fixed in far-back days, has found it natural and easy to adjust his thoughts to the new knowledge of today. He recognizes that, come whatever turnings may, there is the same God at the heart of things, the same human needs and inspirations, the same yearning for light upon the way of life.[156]

Thayer then systematically parted from Vickers and Wendte and, point by point, outlined his Unitarian beliefs. The Trinity he rejected not by recourse to Arian or Socinian definitions but because there are no reliable and authoritative biblical documents that verify such division of God: "...the Procession of the Holy Spirit, the Consubstantiality of the Son with the Father, the Double Nature and the Two Wills in Christ have altogether lost their vitality to any but the antiquarian." The term Son of God is then put into context by stating that, in a sense, all are considered sons of God. For Unitarians, the application of the term only to Jesus is meaningless. Thayer then compared his view of the Bible to those of other faiths and scholars, and he concluded that it is a mixture of the true and untrue:

The Bible is a collection of books of unequal merits. It is literature to be understood and digested, not dogma to be received in fear and trembling; its science is old-fashioned and out of date, its piety, where it reaches the serene heights of trust and awe, is perennially quickening to all which is best in the soul. We Unitarians, therefore, select of its morsels of wisdom that which is of high quality,…that which stirs the best sentiments of the conduct of life; some chapters we read often and with fondness; others are not fit to be read in church, nor suitable for anybody but the antiquarian or the philosopher.[157]

He asserted that twentieth century Unitarians believed that Jesus was naturally born and mortal, and the last in the line of Jewish prophets described in the Old Testament. Thayer also adopted the transcendental beliefs of Emerson and Parker, rejecting the miracles of the New Testament, but he was unsure of the validity of the title of Messiah taken during Jesus' lifetime and in later versions of the gospels. However, he rejected the concept of Jesus the Messiah as "a superhuman being, far removed from any place among men who have moved in history." He then used the central issues of religion, the nature of God and the after-life, to define his theology. Postulating that Unitarians do not call any faith false, he expressed the belief that all humans have a sense of morality and reverence for life that can be defined as religion. When these are expressed in the Bible it becomes a religious instrument. Where sacred books of other faiths demand such behavior, they too must be accepted as religious and relevant. As he put it: "Whatsoever in a national literature promotes righteousness and good will is inspiring, and, therefore, inspired scripture." Unitarians generally had difficulty in expressing their belief in God. Thayer started by addressing the "Uni:" "The All-Power is one and not many." Anticipating the late twentieth century thrust for gender neutrality, he then expresses God as "He or She, Infinite father and Mother… immanent, ever-present, working by uniform laws which intelligence can discover." For Unitarians prayer was a conversation between the human soul and God, not to request material things or well being but rather a hope for the ability to achieve tranquility and peace of mind. Immortality was rarely discussed in Unitarian services outside of memorial celebration of life for the deceased. Thayer though added another dimension to the term, postulating that all religions believe that the soul survives even after death. Unitarians felt that man, as a son of God, was imperishable just as God is but rejected the concept of heaven or hell as reward or punishment for mortal actions. In death the body that housed the soul might perish but the soul would continue as a spirit.

As much as Unitarians abhor a creed, Thayer at the end of his sermon established a credo that could well be accepted by theists one hundred years later:

> I believe in God, the unbounded wisdom, love and power.

> I believe in God's ever-renewed revelation of truth and duty, to which each generation of man in history makes some contribution.

> I believe that the main evidence that any race of individuals is divinely inspired is in its service of humanity. Wheresoever good will and good works are, there is the love of God manifest towards his children.

> I believe in the eventual victory of knowledge, right and justice over all which now hinders their prosperity.

> I believe that as God is perfect, in the process of the ages the perfect truth and love will be willingly received into all minds in time or in the unseen world.

> I believe in one God, one law, one element and one far-off divine intent, to which the whole creation moves.

Thayer's theist theology was well accepted by the city's population that took pride in the diversity of the First Church population and attracted high ranking politicians to its services. Most notably the Tafts were members and in 1909 William Howard Taft became president of the United States. Later he became chief justice of the Supreme Court. Taft did not enjoy being president, particularly dealing with a reluctant congress, and he turned to Unitarianism for solace. Also in 1909 Taft was the principal founder of the National League of Unitarian Laymen and honorary president of the organization. During his presidency, he regularly attended All Souls Church in Washington, a source of relief and spiritual support. In 1919, now retired from the presidency, Taft addressed the General Conference of Unitarians and other Liberal Christian Churches and defined his theology. He titled his lengthy discourse *The Religious Convictions of an American Citizen* and, like many Unitarian ministers, felt it necessary to explain what Unitarianism meant:

> Now, what are Unitarians? Are they Christians? Of course, that is a matter of definition. If a man can be a Christian only when he believes in the literal truth of the creed as it is recited in the orthodox evangelical churches, then we Unitarians are not Christians. A Unitarian believes that Jesus Christ founded a new religion and a new religious philosophy on the love of God for man, and of men for one another, and for God, and taught it by his life and practice, with such Heaven-given sincerity, sweetness, simplicity, and all-compelling force that it lived after him in the souls of men, and became the basis for a civilization struggling toward the highest ideals. Unitarians, however, do not find the evidence of the truth of many traditions which have attached themselves to the life and history of Jesus to be strong enough to overcome the presumption against supernatural intervention in the order of nature. They feel the life of Jesus as a man to be more helpful to them, as a religious inspiration, than if he is to be regarded as God in human form. They find in the higher criticism of the Gospels reason enough to explain those passages in which

the supernatural is set forth as part of Jesus life and doctrine, as additions to a much simpler story upon which the synoptic gospels were founded. They learn that the composer of each gospel had a bent and a motive which colored his rendition of an earlier story, and that the prompting to do so was found in early controversies in the Church between Jews and Gentiles. They realize that the grandness of style and the doctrinal character of the Fourth Gospel were well suited and were necessary to the strengthening of the Christian Church, as it then was, among the people of the civilized world. But they deny that they lose the essence of Christianity when they give up miracles, the Virgin birth, and the deity of Jesus. The Unitarians have always emphasized the life of Jesus in his teaching of love as the foundation of all things spiritual, and the motive and end of the Kingdom of God. In that sense, and that we believe to be the true sense, Unitarians are Christians.[158]

He then underscored the influence of Unitarianism on other denominations:

The views which Unitarians have avowedly adopted as their faith have forced themselves, in one form or another, into the minds of many laymen and some clergymen of orthodox churches. They have softened the rigidity of a narrow insistence on literal acceptance of every dogma. They have liberalized the attitude of many of the evangelical churches. Many orthodox clergymen have done away largely with the doctrinal sermon and with attacks upon differing creeds. Instead they exalt, as they should, the profoundly helpful example of Jesus' life and his pregnant parables and lessons of love and true happiness in seeking the Kingdom of God. They dwell upon the purpose of all his actions, embodied in the sentence: "And Jesus went about doing good."

Not only that, but they are making their churches centers of doing good. They are showing the essence of Christianity by their works of helpfulness. Many modern churches have become institutional in the organization of branches for philanthropic, charitable and educational progress among those for whom they feel responsible. While I do not say that this change indicates a general surrender by church authorities of the tenets of the orthodox Christian creed, it indicates a change of emphasis that enables many laymen to remain within the church whose minds tend toward a more liberal Christianity. This change has, I believe, strengthened the churches in their useful and elevating influence upon society, and it has brought all churches' closer together in a common advance. There is more team work among them.[159]

Taft spoke not as former United States president but as a layman, a Unitarian, who had faith in the power of religion for the good of mankind.

Despite Taft's association, the Cincinnati church influence waned under Alson Robinson. His deep pacifism during World War I conflicted with the views of many members, and he was forced to resign less than one year into his tenure. In 1918 John Malick followed as minister of the congregation and remained for twenty years, but his ministry came to an abrupt end after he divorced his wife and married a member of the church choir. After regret and debate, Reverend Malick was asked to resign.

Cincinnati Unitarianism was not isolated to the two major churches, a fact that is relatively unknown in the denomination. Rejected by the American Unitarian Association, a small group of African Americans under the leadership of William Henry Grey Carter founded the Church of the Unitarian Brotherhood in Cincinnati's West End, the poorest part of the city. Church membership never seemed to rise above sixty members, yet Carter continued to hold services advocating faith in the oneness of God, as well as a God of love and reason. As Reverend Sharon Dittmar, the current minister of Cincinnati's First Unitarian Church, put it: "He was a minority within a minority within a minority. His race made him a minority within the country, his faith made him a minority within the black community, and his race made him a minority within Unitarianism." Despite its rejection by the national Unitarian movement, Carter's church existed on its own for more than twenty years. It would do so through the years of the great depression. In January 2001, Dittmar, held a Service of Commemoration and Reconciliation honoring the descendants of the first minister of that church. In her sermon she apologized for the neglect of this congregation. She exposed the sad fact that, as late as the 1930s, Unitarians clung to their elite, white, well-educated, and upper middle class status. First Church did make a conscious decision to remain in its building on Linton Street in the Avondale section of Cincinnati, a space it had occupied since 1888 despite the fact that the neighborhood was no longer as affluent as it once was. This paralleled the decision of the Saint Louis First Unitarian Church to remain in a mid-town area of the city rather than move to the suburbs.

According to Cincinnati church history, the modern era of the congregation began with the arrival of Ellsworth Smith in 1939. He was followed by Robert O'Brien. In the spectrum of Unitarian beliefs, Smith was a theist with a tinge of Humanism but not in the rigid doctrinaire sense of Dietrich, while O'Brien was the exact reverse. Both left the definition of religious words such as *God* or *Faith* to each individual, and both sermonized about Unitarian beliefs and social values while trying to explain how a non-creedal church could still be deeply religious. Smith did this by addressing, in a series on the Unitarian Faith, how the "Bibles of the World" and prayer related to liberal Unitarians. His thesis was that Americans believe that the Bible was the word of God, and those reading it for a revealed truth cannot find one or understand it. He then clearly delineated a modern Unitarian view of the scriptures:

> The Bible is a disappointing book to many. A man consumed by a spiritual need to find saving truth, buys a Bible and then becomes puzzled by what he reads. All too often people buy Bibles, give up trying

to understand them, then put them on a shelf, their spirits frustrated but their sense of holiness of the Bible unimpaired. I suppose that the same is true of other religions...

This is how the Bibles of the world were written [by word of mouth passed from generation to generation]. They are not the accurately dictated words of supernatural authorities, but the accumulated legends of wondrous things that happened in the past. The marvel is that they contain so much material of such splendid worth. Unitarians who, in general, do not accept the Bible or any other written document as having authority over them, nevertheless yield to no one in the appreciation of the values that are to be found in our Bible and the Bibles of other religions. The Bibles of the world record the activities and the words of people considered divine. In many cases these people did not consider themselves divine but quite ordinary people with a need to communicate to others their concerns and their insights... We cloak the heroes with mantles of divinity because we have been so encouraged, helped by them that we think them above the ordinary. We do this also for a subtler reason – that we do not wish to compare ourselves in our dullness and predilections to failure with these inspiring and shining creatures, so we call them divine. We deify our religious heroes by a slow process of believing all that is wonderful about them that has been told us and then passing on the narrative enhanced by our own admiring touches and eventually forgetting the less admirable, until after a few generation our descendants envision a very holy creature indeed, one with many miraculous qualities and no faults.

Smith then differentiated the biblical accounts of Jesus from those of Saint Paul, the latter more dominant in traditional Christian denominations. He maintained that the rejection of conventional Christianity and acceptance by some of the religion of Jesus was central to Unitarianism. Prayer was another sermon subject. Smith's belief was that prayer may have been too narrowly defined. It should not just be part of a worship service but, more often, could be a deep meditation. In his words: "For me prayer has become more meaningful since I no longer seek...the attention and approval of a God whom I hope to persuade to help me." He contended that prayer is a natural outcome of one's emotions:

> I say that whenever I feel a strong surge of moral, ethical or spiritual which, like the magnetic force of an electrical field, organizes and draws into a pattern the scattered emotions of my life, I believe I am experiencing prayer. Sometimes it is a passing mood, sometimes it dominates a day and gives it a special quality, and sometimes it becomes a turning point, a mutation of my life...Prayer is not the noting of outward appearance but the sensing of inward realities. Prayer is sensitivity, apprehension, awareness, caring. Prayer, then is a very social thing – it binds us close to each other. It is the "tie that binds our hearts in mutual love," it is the "fellowship of kindred souls" and the discovery that all souls are kindred in the real confrontation of life. The thankfulness we feel in prayer is the simple gladness at the miracle that permits us really to sense the other person's joy or sorrow, hope or despair, and thus assures us that we belong to each other more truly than we belong to ourselves alone.

Ellsworth Smith's sermons were those of an optimist who searched for a good life. In January 1957 he addressed the issue of why humans are on earth in a sermon called *The Search for Meaning*:

> The philosophers...are the ones who take most seriously the old injunction "Oh Man, Know thyself!" The poets seek answers in their forms, the artists and

musician in theirs. Political and economic systems, by experiment and demonstration seek to provide some answers. The mystic has his own way of seeking, which he can scarcely communicate to others. It used to be said that theology was the queen of the sciences. It never was. But it may well be that the man of religion, schooled in an understanding of the implications of all the other fields of knowledge, has the responsibility to answer the question "Why?" the question "What is the meaning?" And it is certainly true that, with many false moves and often operating on false basic premises, the man of religion has been giving full time to the all-embracingness of the search for meaning. Religion cannot help being, particularly if liberally defined, the central search for meaning.

If I have one solid, basic religio-philosophical belief, it is that which is necessary in the long run is good and that it will eventually come to pass. This statement has vast implications. What is necessary means here what is necessary for the spirit and survival of man. What is good here means that goodness in this case refers to man's survival and meaning. Will come to pass is not just an expression of hope – it is my belief that mankind on this earth will persist, though civilizations yet fail – that evolution has gone far enough to assure a species adaptable enough to meet the exigencies of the future. What is necessary is good and it will come to pass.

It is clear that Ellsworth Smith talked about religion in very personal terms. His sermons expressed deep feelings and celebrated life.

In late 1957, Robert O'Brien took over the ministry, and remained at First Church for five years. His sermons reflected life experiences and encounters and often were more philosophical than religious. A Catholic as a child, he became interested in Unitarianism and became a minister. He freely admitted that he did not believe in God, and he found it necessary to define the relation between minister and congregation in great detail. In his 1959 sermon he tried to explain his humanist philosophy using an analogy to the sixteenth century philosopher Erasmus, who was a thorn in the side of the Catholic Church and writer of the great satire *In Praise of Folly*. Said O'Brien:

> In considering matters theological, I hope we count ourselves among the students of Erasmus; it is so easy to worship the goddess of Folly while believing that one is seeking some ultimate truth. I am not sure that Ecclesiastics or Koheleth, as it is in the Old Testament, was right when he said that "there is nothing new under the sun"... Certainly there is reason for us to believe that man has always pondered the question of his origin, the nature and meaning of his destiny and the conditions of his existence. These are theological problems; these are ancient problems and they are inescapable. Newton charted the course of the stars in terms of celestial mechanics; Einstein has given us insight into other dimensions of the universe. The difference lies not in the stars themselves, but in the view of man. The schoolmen of the Catholic Church, the apologists of its doctrine tried to prove the existence of God by logic and by creed. Today logic is the servant of empirical science, and creed is no longer founded upon unquestioned authority. We, as Unitarians, have no theology of God; no system of beliefs to which all of us must subscribe. There are Unitarians who believe in the more traditional Christian meaning of God as a person – not as a physical person, but fulfilling the principle of person. The personalistic theism of Christianity is represented among many Unitarians. There are Unitarians on the other side, who have abandoned all references to the meaning of God, feeling that it is so crowded with difficulties and

ambiguities that it confuses rather than enlightens our discussion.

In his 1961 sermon, *The Preacher and I, Reflections on the Liberal Ministry*, he discussed the effect of a non-creedal denomination on the ministry:

> Our liberal ministry is not only a difficult profession; it is essentially an impossible one. He cannot claim to be a "man of God", for he knows that he is a man of history. To him doubt must be as important as faith. He is both minister and self. As minister he seeks to become what he cannot hope to be, as self he must forgive his failures. He is the preacher and the "I". A minister must always realize that there will be a group within his congregation who are waiting for him to leave, and among, those who complain of his preaching, will be some who have never heard him speak, (A minister once said that his congregation was 100% behind him – 50% for him and 50% against.) A minister must always be prepared for disappointment,

Yet this doubt and pessimism belies O'Brien's ministry in Cincinnati. These were the 1960s, and the Vietnam War was at the foreground of a divided country. There was no doubt where O'Brien stood: he was a peace activist who participated in many protests and once was even arrested. In 1962, he returned to the subject of Christianity and world conflict in a sermon titled *What I Expect from my Religion*:

> Unitarianism is an open faith which has no prescribed creed. What I say this morning about my expectation of my religion must, of necessity, be a personal confession. First of all I expect my religion to remind me that I am responsible for the fate of my fellow human beings. Judaism teaches that "God hath made of one blood all nations of men to dwell on the face of the earth." The apostles of the New Faith declared: "In Christ there is no East or West."

These are the pronouncements of our religion, yet they are not our common practice, and we know wherein we are wrong. If we consult the Christian doctrine, it proclaims that the church "is the body of Christ in the world". In this sense the church has no self-interest; it is not corruptible because it is not attached to anything in this world. Its ultimate reason transcends the world...Almost nowhere has Christianity been able to liberate men from their parochial culture, nor has it lifted us above our self-occupations. The church has not been capable of taming the nations. For example, at the recent World Council of Churches meeting which was aimed at uniting all of Christendom, no pronouncement was made against the nations that are now arming themselves with weapons which could ultimately destroy human life. It may be asking the impossible to expect nations to conduct themselves in accordance with moral precepts, yet I fail to see how the Church can ask for anything less. Christianity has given the sanctions to the conduct of the West, Marxism has given its sanction to the ambitions of the Soviet Union, and between the two the moral terms are ambiguous.

He went on to say that he expected Unitarianism to praise the ordinary things in daily life and to hold people morally responsible for society as a whole. "I want to be inspired not only by familiar ceremonies but also what has the power to astonish me." He ended with this summary:

I have not stated all of my expectations of religion, yet I am sure there will be those of you who will say that I am expecting too much already. But my defense lies in the fact that religion is worthy only of unreasonable expectations, and to the degree that we settle for less we forget that religion represents man's self-surpassing nature, and that it is the source of prophetic sight which makes all advances in

87

human destiny possible. I know the limitations of my religion, and yet I look to it for help to find a way to live which I could not find without it.

It is hard to discern a distinct theology in O'Brien's writings. While he denied the pure humanism of Reese and Dietrich, there were equally strong denials of theism and no expression of how he defined a religious center. When he left the Cincinnati church in 1962, he left a congregation divided as to what it should expect of a new minister.

It chose James Hutchinson who faithfully served First Church from 1963 to1971. He was a scholar, described as brilliant, a subtle curmudgeon and a stickler for grammar. He left First Church in 1971 because there had been growing unhappiness with his ministry and until Sharon Dittmar was appointed in 1998, four ministers were called to First Church in a period of twenty-seven years. Not counting interim ministers, their average tenure was no more than six years.

Dittmar, the current pastor, is a graduate of Harvard Divinity School and a progressive liberal. In her sermons she specifically addresses concern for minorities, women and the poor. Her theology is best illustrated in a September 2000 sermon titled *Images of God* in which describes her own journey to Unitarianism. She applauds the introduction of gender inclusive language in worship services and prayer books, as well as softened interpretations of formerly rigid theological concepts like predestination and salvation. Dittmar classes herself as a pantheist, defined as an ever-present God, but one that cannot be known by man. Her theological statement is reminiscent of the views of Ellsworth Smith.

Beyond her extensive sermonizing, in 2007 Dittmar was able to establish a meaningful mission statement for the church:

> We, the members of First Unitarian Church of Cincinnati, promise one another to work together toward achieving these objectives:

> Celebrating Our Community:

> To nurture a caring and welcoming community.

To seek more diversity in our community and to expect every church committee to promote inclusion.

To empower congregants to make a difference in the life of the church.

To explore weeknight activities that build community and facilitate committee work.

To encourage all congregants to participate actively in membership growth.

To put into place an ongoing communications strategy for membership growth.

To build and maintain warm cooperative relationships with Unitarian Universalist churches locally, regionally and continentally.

Seeking Our Spiritual and Ethical Paths:

To reach out to persons looking for a religious community like ours.

To encourage congregants to be open to ideas and philosophies different from their own.

To provide high-quality religious/ethical education for children, youth and adults in the congregation and the community.

To renovate our building so that it enhances our worship, honors our history and welcomes all.

To enrich our own spiritual experience with a diversified arts program.

Working for Justice:

To explore the responsibilities of being an urban Unitarian Universalist church in the 21st century.

To focus on social justice programs where we can be most effective.

To live in harmony with nature, recognizing the interconnectedness of all life.

This statement is religiously neutral. It indicates openness to any theology without mentioning words like Faith, God or a Higher Spirit. The Cincinnati church thus accommodates the diverse views of the national Unitarian movement in general and its urban environment in particular. In this, it differs markedly from Saint Louis's First Unitarian Church. From very similar origins these two churches diverged theologically in the mid-twentieth century and today have very different belief systems.

Unitarianism in Saint Louis.

Saint Louis was founded in 1763 by French explorers who came south on the Mississippi River and formed a small settlement. Another French group under Lassale came north from Louisiana to join them. A Catholic church was established in 1763 and during the eighteenth century, the area's population was largely Catholic. In 1803, the territory was ceded to the United States through the Louisiana Purchase, and, in 1821 Missouri became the twenty-fourth state admitted to the Union. By 1835, when the Church of the Messiah was formed, Saint Louis had only 7,500 inhabitants, but unrest in Western Europe in 1848 spurred immigration and immigrants arrived from Germany and Italy. Missouri was a free state, but on the border between the slaveholding south and the free north. By1833, Unitarianism had spread as far west as Saint Louis at a time when immigrants who came to Saint Louis were generally young, enterprising and liberal. William Greenleaf Eliot stated that they were not very religious and generally from the middle or poorer classes. This may be why perhaps they were open to inclusive Arminianism, and accepted the freedom of non-creedal religions more readily than older residents of the area.

Among these early settlers were a few New Englanders who had been exposed to Unitarianism and were ready to form a church and attract a minister. Leaders of the movement were Christopher Rhodes, James Smith, and George H. Callender, the last a business owner in Saint Louis who came from a prominent family. These men began to advertise in New England for someone who might be persuaded to come to Saint Louis. In 1833, Rhodes travelled east to the Harvard Divinity School to interview graduates. William Greenfield Eliot, with great trepidation, accepted the invitation and brought Unitarianism to Saint Louis.

It was not the first time that Unitarianism had been preached in the city. As early as 1830, John Pierrepoint came from Boston to speak about the movement at the Market House. In 1833 George Chapman, a Unitarian minister from the Louisville church, came to Saint Louis three times and preached at the National Hotel. As described in chapter two, in 1832 Louisville had attracted Harvard Divinity School graduate James Freeman Clarke, who was Eliot's good friend and confidant. Clarke had informed Eliot of the opening, who was then contacted by the Saint Louis group and offered the position. Thus it was to Clarke that Eliot turned for advice, not just for an assessment of whether Saint Louis could sustain a Unitarian church, but, more importantly, to receive guidance on the fundamental question of theology. For as late as November 1833, Eliot was questioning his religious orientation. He wrote to Clarke: "Suppose that I devote two years to the judicious study of philosophy and explore the mores of transcendentalism – I may end dreaming, a skeptical or mystical being.... What is man without faith?"[160] He went on to express his doubts: "Came to the conclusion that there is one philosophy, one religion and only one. What they are God only knows." But he soon resolved these questions by accepting theist beliefs with an Arminian orientation, rejecting the idea that God "sports with our weaknesses and mocks our poor efforts." God was to him a loving power, and man alone was responsible for his utterances and thoughts.

In February 1834, Eliot was seriously considering the Saint Louis offer and made inquiries as to the prospects of success, the character of the people, and the probable number of Unitarians. One month later he made up his mind to go west. He was ordained in August and set out on his journey through Pittsburgh and Louisville, arriving on November 27, 1834. Three days later, he preached his first sermon in Elihu Sheperd's school rooms and attracted so many for the afternoon service that more than one hundred were left outside. The city then offered the Court House and City Hall, but after two more Sunday services, lawyers representing traditional Christian denominations objected to this use of public facilities. Presbyterians, Methodists, Episcopalians, and Catholics all denounced him "with a great deal of bitterness," and after orthodox lawyers circulated a petition to eject him from these venues, it became clear that Unitarians had to build a church. Rhodes and Callender immediately began to raise money for this and managed to collect six hundred dollars the first day. Until the church was built services were held in the Masonic Hall. According to Earl Holt, the projected cost of a simple building would be seventeen thousand dollars, of which three thousand was raised in Saint Louis. [161] He also maintains that when the first church building was dedicated in October 1837, the congregation incurred a large debt. A slightly different picture is given by Eliot, who tried to raise money in New England churches. On May 10, 1835, he preached in Boston and stated that two-thirds of the sum required for the building was obtained from Unitarians and friends in Saint Louis. An additional two thousand dollars was required to "avoid involving us in a burdensome debt and the attendant troubles." With interest at the time at more than ten percent, Eliot made a remarkably modern plea for funds: "We cannot pay two hundred to three hundred dollars interest and also pay for the required general expenses of the church." In his sermon he called the Saint Louis Unitarians "now a small and feeble society." He made the case that a single church in Saint Louis, from its central position, its large mobile population, and its vicinity to many places where Unitarianism could be established, would be "a great good." The 1881 history of the Church of the Messiah is specific; the church cost was twelve thousand dollars, with five thousand raised in St. Louis, three thousand from eastern churches, and a loan for four thousand dollars. Eliot, in his plea for funds in Boston, laid a foundation for the principle that older churches had a responsibility to propagate Unitarianism by supporting fledgling congregations. He would be active in aiding mid-western and southern churches throughout his life.

The Church of the Messiah under Eliot's direction practiced Christian Unitarianism untainted by transcendentalism. Earl Holt's seminal work on Eliot covers his activities in Saint Louis. He calls him a Conservative Radical. Certainly his conservative theology was solidly founded on the Harvard Divinity School teachings of Henry Ware and Ellery Channing. Eliot had left Boston before the Unitarian controversy erupted in earnest. (Emerson's Divinity School Address was given in 1838 and Parker's sermon on the Transient and the Permanent in Christianity was preached in 1848.) In the decade preceding Eliot's arrival in Saint Louis, however, the controversy about the authenticity of biblical miracles had occupied New England Unitarian ministers as well as Harvard Divinity School faculty, and graduates were found on both sides of the debate. The *Christian Examiner and Register* published critical articles about the claims of divine intervention in the Old Testament and the miracle stories of the New Testament. With Eliot's extensive correspondence and visits to New England, he must have been keenly aware of the burgeoning controversy.

His involvement in social and civic affairs was rooted in the training received at the Divinity School. According to William A. Deiss of the Smithsonian Institution Archives, Henry Ware had encouraged his students to participate in the Philanthropic Society, an organization devoted to a vigorous discussion of moral values of American life, including slavery, intemperance, poverty, and Sunday schools. While still a student, Eliot was particularly interested in prison reform, and he visited prisons, hospitals and asylums. [162] Eliot maintained his theological conservatism, but his radicalism came to the fore through his civic work in Saint Louis. Earl Holt aptly titled his discussion of Eliot's activities *The Whole City Was His Parish*. In 1847, Eliot travelled to Europe for the first time. Through his contacts with English Unitarians, Eliot undoubtedly became aware of their intense involvement in political and civic affairs as exemplified by the Christian Social Movement of Maurice and Solly, then just in its infancy. On his return in 1848, he joined the Saint Louis school board and immediately realized that the schools were in most respects substandard. His solution was first to import teachers from New England and then to increase school funding by using tax revenue. A bill was passed by the state legislature and submitted to voters in 1849, in effect creating one of the first publicly financed school systems in the nation.[163] Yet 1849 would become a disastrous year for Saint Louis. January saw the death of the first victim of cholera, a disease that would ravage the city and kill ten percent of its population. In May a barge fire on the Mississippi spread to buildings on the Missouri shore and destroyed a large portion of the city. It was brought under control only by destroying houses along streets fronting the river. According to Holt, four hundred buildings were lost and the total damage exceeded six million dollars.[164] In such a climate, voters were reluctant to pass any tax increase but, in spite of general opposition, the bill was passed through the efforts of the membership of the Church of the Messiah who mobilized voters through a door to door canvass.

Of huge importance for today's Saint Louis was the 1853 action of one of Eliot's parishioners to charter the Eliot Seminary. When the incorporators met for the first time a year later, they felt that it was inappropriate to use Eliot's name for a future school of higher learning and that the school should devote its curriculum to more than religion. The institution was renamed Washington Institute, later to become Washington University in Saint Louis. Education was Eliot's main occupation while still ministering to the Church of the Messiah. He founded the Mission Free School to support the education of indigent children and orphans. Eight years later he founded the Western Sanitary Commission. In 1870, he was appointed Acting Chancellor of Washington University and had to curtail his work as a minister severely.

Only in one respect did Eliot fail to reflect a Unitarian issue of his time, and that was his silence on the subject of slavery. As discussed in chapter two, by 1850 the topic was uppermost in the minds of most Unitarian ministers in the East and as far west as Cincinnati. Conway had preached his abolitionist sermon of *East versus West* and accepted the fact that members of his congregation disagreed with him so strongly that they formed a splinter church. Eliot was reluctant to take that chance. Missouri was a border state, but the Missouri Compromise of 1820 sanctioned it as a slave-owning state. Some Unitarians owned slaves while others were abolitionists. Before the start of the Civil War, Eliot took refuge in his determination not to inject politics in his sermons. By 1861, he felt it was necessary to speak out. While he firmly supported the Union and deplored secessionists, he remained mute on the subject of slavery.

Eliot's theology is evident in a sermon preached on Easter Sunday. His theme was Jesus as our Lord, our Redeemer and our High Priest, yet he called him the Man from Calvary. Resurrection meant that the spirit triumphed over death and the risen Christ was an expression of that faith. Eliot's notes elaborated on this theme. The purpose of Christ's coming was an augmentation of prophecies, to establish God as the father to all yet also as the savior of man. Jesus communicated to the world the things he had been taught by God, and also revealed Him to be pardoning humankind, in effect the instrument of man's reconciliation with the infinite. Yet as conservative as Eliot was in his Christianity, one finds strong evidence that he believed that free will was a necessary ingredient in religion. As he wrote in 1833: "Let us all admit into our mind the idea of God as of not one who sports with our weaknesses and mocks at our poor efforts, but as a dear God who made and loveth all. We are responsible for all we do and say and think."[165] Later he elaborated on his beliefs: "We are Unitarians because we believe in the unbroken Unity of God. We love the name because it represents the movement frankly. We are pledged to no sect and are slaves to no party. But we must be Christians." He echoed Channing that there is no assertion of Christ's divinity in the gospels. In an 1864 sermon, Eliot expressed this Unitarian belief: "A careful examination of their [the apostles] words, however, shows that they never forgot the difference between the Father and the son, between the ambassador and the Sovereign who sends him, between the mediator who effects the reconciliation and the infinite."[166]

Eliot considered the educational function of the church very important. In October 1848 he outlined why a young man should learn religion. At the top of the list was the ability of religion to teach "restraint inward over passions and appetites." Next came an almost puritan stricture to guard against the temptation of the world, followed by providing guidance in choosing the right path of life. Only then, almost as an afterthought, did he mention "for his salvation." He quoted the gospel of John with its many references to Jesus but always called him the son of man. Eliot felt that transcendentalism erred in doubting the existence of God. As he put it: "One cannot explain the spread of Christianity without a divine mission. Is it that we doubt the existence of God or has our belief in him become so cold and abstract under the name of philosophical or transcendental, that its vitality is all gone?" In 1868 he published a volume on the *Doctrines of Christianity* and described the Bible as presenting to contemporary man both a mystery and a number of contradictions. Thus it was not an infallible revealed text: "Christianity never tells us to stop thinking, but to prove all things and hold fast what is good."[167] In an obvious reference to the transcendental controversy, he asserted that the outcry of many traditional Unitarians against reason was "not only unwise but also inconsistent with their own practice." Unitarians should be able to accept the plain and direct meaning of the Bible more than other Christians. There was no doubt, in Eliot's mind that Jesus was a man who prayed to God and did so as an act of submission. The mystery of the holy spirit was explainable as a manifestation of God's spirit in man, not as a third entity: "To deny the personality of the Holy Spirit separate from that of the Father is not to deny the Holy Spirit itself...In God we live and move and have our being. He works within us both to will and to do of his good pleasure. He is more ready to give his Holy Spirit to those that ask him than an earthly parent is to bestow good things upon his children."[168]

In his 1860 notebook one finds the draft of a creed, encompassing a belief in goodness as embodied in the life of Christ, with his life an example rather than a doctrine. Eliot deemed it essential to be truthful and, in a departure from orthodox Unitarianism, he stressed the need for freedom of belief and the right to differ: "One could say that the Bible is truthful, but who is capable of interpreting it."[169] In 1864 he defined his own view of the role of preachers: "I would not for the world feel that the great truths of religion depend on their certainty ...solely on my own speculations. It is true that they are rational conclusions and the more we study them the more perfectly they seem in accordance with the natural laws of thought…Natural religion, so called, culminates in the divine."[170] In saying this Eliot came dangerously close to Parker's concept of absolute religion.

Eliot did not believe that Universalism was equivalent to Unitarianism, because the former expanded the benevolence of God [by saving all souls regardless of sin], and pointing out, [in Unitarianism] that to be just, this benevolence requires goodness on the part of man. In many of Eliot's writings, one finds a strong emphasis on the role of conscience, the conviction that humans are aware of their transgressions, and that man would be held responsible for his actions. In his theology, universal salvation was replaced by the need for atonement. Almost as an afterthought Eliot added that he believed God to be merciful. Eliot's effectiveness can be measured by attendance numbers. In 1835, when he came to Saint Louis, after an initial surge of curiosity seekers, eight people were in attendance. In 1836, the Sunday school of the church had eight teachers and eight or nine children all offspring of the sexton. By 1839, the church employed its first religious educator, Seth A. Ranlett, and "many hundreds came under his care", and by 1851 the church had expanded to its second building at Ninth and Olive Street. Thirteen hundred came to its dedication of which two hundred fifty were communicants.

In 1873 Eliot decided that his duties as Chancellor of Washington University would prevent him from devoting time to the church, and he requested that the congregation look for another minister. John Snyder took over the pulpit to remain with the Church of the Messiah for twenty-five years. Snyder had a mixed heritage, with German Lutherans on his father's side and Quakers on his mother's. With such a split religious background Snyder turned to Unitarianism, and enrolled in the Meadville Theological School, then still in Pennsylvania. Following his graduation in 1869, Snyder served as pastor for the Unitarian church in Hingham, Massachusetts, until he was called to Saint Louis. He was described as a leader, "famous for the strength, originality, beauty, and timeliness of his pulpit utterances."[171] Eliot's ministry had set very high standards for a young man just four years out of divinity school, but Snyder rose to the occasion. He turned out to be a moral teacher, "head of many movements," and established the general culture and intelligence prevalent in his church. Like Eliot he was active in the political life of the city. Snyder's theology was revealed in an 1899 paper on Unitarianism in Saint Louis. As might be expected of a minister of the Church of the Messiah, he emphasized the unity of God rather than commenting on the transcendentalism that could be found in many Unitarian churches. His theology was also revealed in a paper written in 1899 for the Northern History Company, and published by the Ladies Eliot Alliance, the church's women's organization. In it he stated, "Nothing can be more certain historically than that the primitive Christian Church was essentially Jewish, monotheistic, and Unitarian. Even the fourth gospel, which the hands of biblical criticism is pushing irresistibly into the second century, contains no doctrine of the divine Trinity." It was during his ministry that the tradition of outstanding church music for Saint Louis Unitarian churches was born. Ernest Kroeger was hired as organist. He was the founder of the American Guild of Organists and created the music program for the Saint Louis World's Fair of 1904.

In 1880, the third building of the Church of the Messiah was dedicated. It was located at the corner of Garrison and Locust Streets and built at a cost of $109,000. Noted Unitarians came from the East to join in the celebration. Henry Bellows, minister of All Souls Unitarian Church, gave the dedication sermon and expressed the theology of Unitarian Christians then common in the East. His thesis was that Paul founded Christianity, not Jesus, but the closeness of Jesus to God was the cornerstone of Christianity. Bellows gave the religion a human face. He said that Christianity was a revelation of God's personality and fatherhood, and that Christ was the chief witness for personal immortality, the providential organizer of moral forces and well disposed spirits, in the interest of humanity. In his view, Unitarians did not expect Christianity to be more diverse than life itself, or human nature or world history, and that on it rested the particular blessing of God. Under Snyder's leadership the Eliot Alliance began the tradition of sponsoring a series of programs for adult education. These were evening programs with extensive reading requirements. The church charged one dollar for alliance members, but they could bring a friend for free. This was a high price for its time, and evidence that the church attracted relatively wealthy people. Nevertheless, it was an attempt not only to increase the literary competence of members, but also an interesting tool for building church membership.

John William Day succeeded Snyder in 1898 and continued his ministry until 1924. He was a prolific writer, and the Eliot Alliance again was able to preserve enough of his sermons to assess his theology. He was a Christian Unitarian, but he felt free to analyze the miracles of the Bible. Jesus to him was divine and holy but also a human being, and Day tried to temper the rigorous acceptance of miracles with twentieth century reason. As a thinking human being, he argued one should reject the claim that Jesus walked on water, turned water into wine, passed through closed doors, or rose into the air:

> People know too much. The public schools have been open too long. Science has shown the causes of things too thoroughly. Material events, the wonders that physics shows, the marvels of discovery, are traced back through natural explanations. The mystery at the heart of them is a mystery that knowledge shows, not one that sets a premium on ignorance. The divineness manifested in the world does not contradict our knowledge. Nothing needs to be unreasonable to be sacred. Poor science does not make good religion. To throw aside astronomy, geology, and discredit the senses and the mind, which are God's highest creation, is not to make piety strong and faith sure.
>
> To say that men must believe in Christ in the twentieth century for the sake of things people in the first century believed is to enclose him in the first century where modern people cannot find him. To make divinity rest on unreasonable things is to make it shake when they fall. Shut up your Christ in ideas outside churches have no interest in and you will never reach the outside people with his influence. [172]

These words might have been spoken by Theodore Parker, but they came naturally to Day as he dealt with a new century and the explosion of science and religious thought. Yet these ideas have an uncanny resonance today. Day's theology was designed to appeal not just to those that called themselves Christians, as the term is used today, but rather to the large group that were unchurched and could not accept miracle stories. They were the ones that should be open to a rational belief in God with Christ as human. They were, in other words, potential Unitarians. The relation of man and God was reflected in Day's sermon question: *What would happen if men really believed in a living God?* The implication was that the belief in God was limited to the past: "Think how the belief in God is limited to a particular time, a limited period, a special people, and evidence of His presence is sought, and conclusive evidence of His power located in that time, not in ours... Religion is reminiscent not actual under these conditions. Faith is called on to support the claim that thus God once lived."[173] (As will be described later, that was also the argument that Thaddeus Clark made in 1958.) Day pleaded for humans to find the supernatural in nature and in science, and he deplored a skepticism that asserted there was no God and thus condoned cheating, stealing, envy, and worse. Yet for Day, the positive faith shines through in the end: "For living men to think of God as living no less than they, would bring unconquerable power – no temptation could be victorious, no sorrow unblessed, no effort vain... Only by becoming themselves temples of a living God can men be sure that there is still God living in the universe."[174] Regarding the divinity of Jesus, Day's theology is clear. In his 1907 sermon titled *The Sinlessness of Jesus* one finds a clear expression of his humanity:

> It is only in the...human sense that we can look on Jesus as sinless. James Freeman Clarke once said that he believed in Christ's sinlessness because he had known others to be sinless. No such fact could be isolated. To make it absolutely exceptional is to remove the possibility of demonstration. The best idea of perfection is one that can be proved. If you know people who have proved it, you have in them

the kind of sinlessness which is fulfilled in Jesus. It is the only kind of perfection which gives us any impulse and confidence and inspiration. The women who replied, when told that her ethics would scarcely come up to the example of Jesus, that she did not set herself to be equal to the Almighty God shows how useless that perfection would be which is impossible to be reached. To ascribe it to Christ is to rob him of his highest dignity. The simpler way is better. "He was true in what is in you and me." This gives us hope for man. It changes the doctrine into life. It makes us say "This is what I am trying to do" and makes us want to do it.

A characteristic of the Church of the Messiah that continues to the present First Unitarian Church was the longevity of service of many of its ministers. Eliot arrived in Saint Louis is 1834 and served until 1873. He was followed by John Snyder who occupied the pulpit until 1898. John William Day was next and remained in the post for a quarter century. The exceptions were William Laurence Sullivan, who took over in 1925 and stayed less than three years, and Charles Addison Wing who succeeded Sullivan and served for four years before being replaced by Walter Samuel Swisher.[175]

In 1868 some members of the Church of the Messiah decided that the city could use another Unitarian church, particularly one that would serve those in south Saint Louis. They formed the Church of the Unity and erected a building at Park and Armstrong Avenues, convenient to Southside parishioners. There were factors beyond geography, however, that caused the split, and they are reflected in each church's statement of beliefs. The Church of the Messiah professed that Christ was savior and the Bible divinely inspired. The Church of the Unity had a more transcendental view of religion. Eliot, who remained at the Church of the Messiah, constructed Articles of Agreement for members of his church:

> We who have here subscribed our names associate ourselves as the Body of Communicants ...for the support of the institutions of Christianity and the enjoyment and edifications of its ordinances. We

hereby profess our faith in Jesus Christ as the Son of God and the Savior of Man and acknowledge the Bible as the divinely authorized rule both of faith and practice. We can find no scriptural authority for closing the doors against any who wish to come. It is the Lord's table not ours, and we welcome all in his name.[176]

A very different statement of purposes was expressed in the Order of Service of the Church of the Unity:

The Church of the Unity is making an absolutely sincere effort to promote the highest interests of human life in Saint Louis. It accepts the teachings of Jesus and Paul that religion is a spirit of faith and hope and trust and love. It leaves all matters of doctrine, all historical questions to the decisions of the individual, while it strives to nourish the highest and finest ideals of our race. It seeks to be a powerhouse of the Spirit, the good spirit of goodwill, of reverence for the best, of consecration to truth and service to fellow man.[177]

The result of the split was that Unitarians in Saint Louis were able to choose between Christian Unitarianism and Transcendentalism, between two theologies as well as two locations.

The Church of the Messiah continued to be a force in the city and played an important role in the denomination. This was clearly shown at the celebration of its 100th anniversary in November 1934. The list of attendees included Dr. George Throop, Chancellor of Washington University, Dr. Louis Cornish, President of the American Unitarian Association, and Christopher Rhodes Eliot, representing the family of poet T. S. Eliot and the church's first minister. The Washington University chorus sang, as did the church choir, then directed by Arthur Lieber. Ministers of both Unitarian churches participated. Walter Swisher represented the Church of the Messiah, and George Dodson represented the Church of the Unity. The theology of the Church of the Messiah was demonstrated by the prayer and responses used in the service. Words such as: "O magnifying the Lord with me and let us exalt his name together; for with him is the fountain of life, and in his light shall we see light." And " O thou sole source of peace and righteousness, take now the veil from every heart, and join us in communion with thy prophets and saints who trusted in thee and were not ashamed." It was a Christian Unitarian service, and even though the Church of the Unity had a more liberal cast, Dodson seems to have found no discomfort in participating, in fact giving an address with a title identical to Snyder's – *Unitarian Christianity in Saint Louis.*

By this time the Church of the Unity was also thriving. In 1870 it had called John Calvin Learned as its first minister and he remained there until his death in 1893. Learned came to the ministry through much soul searching and after teaching school in the Ozarks since 1856. In 1859 he entered Harvard Divinity School and graduated in two years. Even though he was acutely aware that Unitarianism was not a dominant religion, he had abandoned the rigor of conventional Christianity, rejecting belief in the Trinity and the divinity of Jesus. A prolific writer, in his essay on Unitarianism he stated that "... no rite is saving or exclusive. The Unitarian believes that God was manifested in Jesus – but that was not the first or last manifestation of the Divine." Learned's theology was transcendental and is best illustrated in his 1883 funeral sermon titled *The Faith of Immortality.* He makes this argument:

> ...the teaching of the doctrine of immortality is but one thing among many duties of even a Christian minister. Those who make it the chief thing, are by no means or by any certainty the best ministers...I assume that this difference about immortality is the same as the differences which men fall into about other religious doctrines – about God and salvation and faith, and heaven and hell, a difference of *words* – which by and by, by a literal and dogmatic use, hide the *things*, and possibly destroy the life for which they stand...But what are the *realities* ? All rational minds give up these – yes, and little by little, as thought matures, give up everything that is found to be perishable, transient and phenomenal. The

more completely the man attains to the spiritual conception, the more is he released from the control of all material imagery... And when we ask concerning the continuance of *personality*, and its security against death, the answer will always depend on the definition we give to this word. Is personality by its nature essential, eternal, or is it phenomenal, something that is wrapped up inseparably, or to be identified with, this perishable body?

When we lay our friend in the grave, it is that which is holiest in our union that rises and asserts itself in new power. His outward form, so dear to our sight, - that we can bear to part from... But the love that underlay these things, the sense the beautiful soul we looked upon, the joy of his happiness, rather than our own – all of this is stronger now than ever. All of this blends with the feeling that what was dearest, best, most personal, self of self, is not extinct, but is more upward. It is that which is lowest and least worthy in our love, to which death comes as a finality. To that in it which is noblest, purest, most worthy to endure, death brings only a new life and consecration.

Learned clearly felt that a funeral should not be a period of mourning but rather a celebration of life. His ministry continued Eliot's tradition for public service. In his January 1884 sermon titled *After Christmas,* he affirmed that society had social needs and that the whole community was responsible for meeting them. He differed from Eliot in one major respect, speaking extensively on the political events surrounding the post Civil War period. Learned's sermons discussed the rise of communism and strongly endorsed capitalism, unusual for a Unitarian minister. His preaching did not so much address a particular theology rather dealing with morality and human rights:"He who disregards human rights has no acceptance with God or Man."

Learned died suddenly in December 1893 and was deeply mourned by the whole Saint Louis community. It fell to his wife

Lucelia to express the depth of Learned's theology in a February 1894 sermon titled *The Ground of a Living Faith*:

> In what can we put the trust of our hearts when sorely tried? How may we gain a faith strong enough to sustain us in times of distraction, sorrow and gloom? – to keep us steadfast when mysteries surround us, calm in the face of loss, willing to live when released from earthly service were easier – confident of truths that we cannot prove ? That which gives us strength, we call faith. It will be easily understood that I am not speaking of faith in a theologic or dogmatic sense; yet to define this sentiment in as little possible as to explain love or to tell what life is. Faith eludes definition; it is more than expectation; it is larger than hope; it is as the New Version has it, "the assurance of things hoped for, the proving of things not seen." It is not knowledge, but it rests on knowledge. It cannot be compelled; it must come in obedience to the call of reason, or by direct insight...
>
> The history of the development of faith in the evolution of the race is the story also in the growth of a single soul. The early races of men lived careless, easy lives; they needed little; that little came with small effort; life was a simple matter; there was death then, and before the vast mystery they stood with cries of terror or in dumb sadness...With later development, with advancing civilization, with the growth of finer sensibilities, of all that gives our life the highest charm, with education came perplexing doubt, obstinate questioning, a great cry from the depth of loss and sorrow, to see the reason of the tangled good and ill; an agonized effort to understand, a longing for some ground of hope that right would prevail, a faith. Years ago all the faiths of the Christian world rested in an infallible man, an infallible church or an infallible book, and the God whom they represented.

This faith was strong; it built noble and enduring lives, but like that of a child, it related almost wholly on outside sources; it demanded little or no activity of mind; it countenanced no individual judgment, and in so far as it did not, it left the intellect a babe-in-arms…

When there comes into the life a love of doing the appointed daily task – however trivial it may seem – however lowly – when there is joy in its faithful performance, straightaway springs up a feeling of kinship will all the ordered processes of nature; we are at once related to the unerring stars that fail not to come nightly in the skies – a conviction fills the soul that it belongs to a divine order – and may be co-worker with God in its creation and development. This is the highest form of worship; it is capable of yielding the same peace – nay, a far deeper peace than formal prayer.

Thus more than a hundred years ago, in a short eulogy, Lucelia Learned expressed the essence of faith voiced in many of today's theist Unitarian churches.

Frederick Lucian Hosmer succeeded Learned as pastor of the Church of the Unity. He was a prolific hymnist and author of much of the music used in churches even today. His ministry was short, only five years, and he was followed by Edward Spencer, and in 1903 by George Rowland Dodson, who remained in this position until the two churches reunited in 1936. A Greek scholar, scientist, and philosopher, Dodson parted from the theological messages of his predecessor by likening religion to nature and science, and he became deeply involved in the politics of this period. His sermon *In Darkest Naturalism and the Way Out* affirmed the changes in the plural character of the world and what constituted faith:[178]

The dire need of this time is for a philosophy that shall legitimate our aspirations and release faith and hope from their imprisonment, and that shall yet be true; for the present generation feels to accept a view of nature and human life which is depressing in that it seems to negate longings that are not only deep, but that we instinctively know to be the noblest part of our environment. The tragedy is that what is noble and divinely beautiful and precious should appear to be untrue. Consider the situation; it is extraordinarily simple and easy to comprehend. Science grows more and ever more comprehensive. It finds natural causes for everything. The heavenly bodies were once supposed to be gods; they are now known to be material masses. Before Kepler's time it was supposed that each planet was guided in its orbital journey by an angel. The angels have all been dismissed and instead we have $mV^2/2$, the formula for work done and energy expended in maintaining the planet's velocity.

…All is natural then? Yes. Including Jesus? Yes, including his life, his love, and his influence in the world. No rose on its stalk, no bird building its nest, no creature fulfilling the law of its being, is more natural than was Socrates drinking the hemlock or Jesus on the rood. From this conclusion there is absolutely no escape. It is only necessary to be clear-headed and see the significance of the truths and principles that we accept without hesitation, in order to have a religion once more. And what a magnificent view that now opens before us for refusing timidly to halt or compromise or attempt to go back! The vision is that of a great process, seemingly material, physical and mechanical in its lower ranges, but evolving at last into a world of conscious, aspiring beings, into faith, hope and love…

On November 15, 1903, Dodson's sermon topic was *The Blending of Ideals*. He remarked that man must rise to fulfill certain ideals in life and this had to be done on his own. There were no mechanical devices to assist him like a cog railway going up or a crane to lift him.

Religion satisfied three great interests of the world – truth or the intellectual, beauty or the aesthetic, and goodness or the moral. The religion of Jesus added the higher life of humanity – the spiritual life. Dodson amplified this essentially Parkerite theology in his address to the Unitarian Ministers Institute, held in Marblehead, Massachusetts on September 28, 1910. His address was titled *The Synoptic Mind; An Ideal of Leadership*:

> ...Jesus is said to have looked on the multitudes with compassion, regarding them as sheep without a shepherd. The situation has improved somewhat [since then], but the multitudes need compassion still. Many of their leaders have lost their way, and are seeking in the forms of pragmatism and other forms of anti-philosophy for humanity's highway. Some have even given up rational ideals, and profess no longer that the universe is an order the truth of which it is possible for us to know. To understand how this disqualifies them for leadership. It is only necessary to remember that all inspiring teaching, every message that has ennobled the lives of men, has been marked by two characteristics, namely, faith in the worth of human nature and in the reality of truth.

> ...There are, then, three great stages in the evolution of thought, namely: 1) The primitive confused awareness, 2) The clearing up of confusion through the making of distinctions, 3) The synoptic view in which things distinguished are seen together.

Dodson went on to say that in traditional religion and education, the nation had not gone beyond the second stage. People separate their thoughts in small compartments that are often confused and treat each as a separate entity. Instead they should accept that true religion enters the third stage where it gathers up all philosophy in one synoptic whole.

The tone of Dodson's sermons hardened in 1911. He openly decried organized labor in a sermon titled *The Menace of Socialism*, railed against the American Socialist Party, and declared war against forced unionization of workers or the closed shop. He thus reflected the views of a congregation that was more upper class and well educated than that of other denominations and one that continued to be a force in the public life of Saint Louis.

In 1916 the Church of the Unity moved from its original location at the corner of Armstrong and Park Avenue to a more central location at 5007 Waterman Avenue. In 1936, the seminal event in Saint Louis Unitarian church life occurred: severe financial problems at the Church of the Messiah forced it to give up its independence. In March, it voted to join the younger congregation to form the First Unitarian Church of Saint Louis. The two combined at the Waterman Avenue location of the Church of the Unity and called its first minister, Laurence Plank. This was not an easy choice. The chosen minister had to accommodate two very divergent views, the Christian Unitarianism of the Church of the Messiah, and an essentially theist and transcendentalist oriented Church of the Unity. Plank fit this role perfectly. While Dodson remained as Minister Emeritus, and represented Unity's theism mixed with a thorough knowledge of science, Plank, a Deist, openly invoked God in his preaching and often referred to the teachings of Jesus. To give him a theological label, he was Socinian with an understanding of the science of his day.

There was no doubt that Plank had a strong grounding in Unitarianism, but he was also a historian. In the three sermons he preached on Unitarianism he went far back into pre-Christian times. He asserted that the first expression of the unity of the deity, which he called "one sublime idea," occurred in 1375 BCE and was made by Ikhnaton, a young Pharaoh who rebelled "against tribalistic priestcraft and authority." Plank amplified his statement: "For the first time in history a universal God is clearly presented. In one of his hymns are the recorded words: "O Thou Only God, there is no other God than Thou." This expression, in a form only slightly modified, is still in use as a Jewish profession of faith. To Plank, Ikhnaton was a precursor of Moses, who in the Old Testament clearly expresses that God and only one God spoke to him in the desert. Thus Moses could be claimed as a Uni-tarian. Plank's deism was encapsulated in the Profession of Beliefs used by the congregation in 1940:

We avow our faith:

In God the Eternal and unconquering love,In the spiritual leadership of Jesus, In the supreme worth of every human personality, In the authority of truth known , or to be known, In the power of good will, In a light of sacrificial spirit to overcome evil, And progressively to establish the kingdom of God. We believe that God is light and that if we walk in the light we will have fellowship with one another. We believe that God fainteth not, nor is He weary; he gives power to the faint and they that wait for him shall renew their strength. We believe in them that love God all things work together for good. We believe that the world passeth away, and the lust thereof, but he who doeth the will of God abideth forever.

This was an explicit deism not encumbered by fear of religious words or references to God and was amplified in a 1942 sermon titled *The Faith and Future of Unitarianism*:

A Unitarian is one whose faith and action are rooted in that kind of religion which releases stimulates and fulfills his own deepest and completest individual being. That his concept of his deepest and central source of all that is, does not detract from this central conviction and emphasis, but rather enriches it and makes it more creative and holy. A Unitarian is distinctive in his religious faith and life in that, to quote the admonition of Jesus, he calls no man master. He is disentangled from all serfdom of mind and heart. He is emancipated from all authoritarianism. He is directly related to his God, and is regimented by no fiats, dogmas and creeds. In his own mind he is free to seek that truth that makes men ever newly and more greatly free. The joyous liberty of the sons of God is his goal, and every existing degree of that liberty he would expand and heighten in himself and others to advance freely toward that grow.

Plank thus delivered the message that joy and faith can and should be part of Unitarianism. His strong deism and sense of celebration was also confirmed in the Unitarian equivalence of baptism that he called *Our Service of Christening and Dedication*. It started with the declaration out of the Hebrew liturgy: "Hear, O Israel, our God is one Lord; and thou shalt love the Lord thy God with all thy heart and with all thy soul and all thy mind." This statement affirmed the Unitarian postulate of God with Jesus as human and avoided any reference to a God-like holy spirit. The dedication finished with a prayer: "Holy and Infinite One, source and goal of all our love and devotion, in Thy name we welcome these little ones, and pray that they, in common with thy children everywhere, may grow in love, that with strength and joy of body, mind, and soul they shall so live as to be a blessing to man and a joy to Thee forever and ever."

When Plank retired in 1945 the church needed a minister. One would have assumed that the search would be for someone with a theology that would continue his deism. The person selected, Thaddeus Clark, was far from that, and yet he would hold the position for twenty-four years. Clark was more philosopher than pastor and much more humanist than previous Saint Louis Unitarian clerics. The contrast between Plank and Clark was so striking that it validates the earlier thesis of this work: the Unitarianism preached in any given church reflects, within limits, the beliefs of the minister rather than those of his congregation. Clark's 1965 Easter sermon is humanist and best illustrates his personal orientation. It is devoid of any reference to the resurrection, God, or Jesus, and is titled *The Right to Believe*:

> Easter has come again and brings with it the promise of life everlasting. It would be inaccurate, however, to say that man has always believed in immortality. It suggests that man somehow can face death only by grasping at the hope of life after death. One of the great refutations of this thesis is to be seen among the Hindus .One of the great histories of religion stated that the Hindu anxiety was not over death, but over

the prospect of the everlasting rebirth which doomed a man to live through an eternal cycle of lives. Every Hindu religion is based upon a prescription that shows a way to escape the endless rebirth'

The question that I should like to raise with you this morning is the propriety of believing in life after death. It is not so much the question of whether we dare believe in afterlife, but whether it is to be permitted. I fear that on this question liberals are much less liberal than on other questions. We are likely to treat those who so believe as if they were willfully deceiving themselves, making them somehow unfit for liberal company...

Our real obligation is the confronting of death that haunts life and, to the Existentialists, reduces life to helpless anxiety. They seem to see the necessary state of man's life as one of anxiety, and this I cannot accept. Death has always confronted man as an inevitable experiment, yet life has continued; and I think we consider death without plunging into anxiety or dread...No, we cannot deny a man the right to believe in immortality; but we do deny, vigorously, that he has the right to demand such belief from us, or that we accept the conclusions he draws from his belief.

Finally Clark got to Easter:

The continuity of life is our ultimate concern, and we see evidence of it on all sides. There is death, to be sure, but there is birth, also. Easter must fall in springtime, for this is a compulsion in man's nature that is older than Easter, older than Christianity – indeed, older than any known religion...Things as they are may not really be bearable if we cannot dream also of things as they ought to be. This is the great dream of humanity, the vision that has drawn men from the slime to walk upright, to make him a noble being in lofty conception and perhaps even fit to dwell with gods.

Not only is there is no hint of theism in his words, there also is little appeal to emotions and no expression of celebration. It is an essay that could be presented on any Sunday in spring. Yet Clark's long tenure in Saint Louis is evidence that the congregation appreciated his scholarly approach to preaching and, while it may have missed an appeal to the emotions, continued to favor his logical approach to religion. At times it was dry, as evidenced in his somewhat circuitous sermon on freedom of religion:

> The elements freedom in our lives and in the universe has left both unfinished and a portion of the work in ours to do. Thus freedom, which we greatly prize, leaves us with an unfinished work so that we are under the necessity of searching. The searching is required by freedom. If there were no real freedom, there would be no searching. And if there is no searching there is no freedom.

> Before us lies the vast unformed future of all time, or that part of it which is ours, and because this is so we can be explorers. The future is open to us as this land was once open to the explorers who came to its shores and moved out through the wilderness and plains. Yet we are not cast merely in the role of explorers. We are more pioneers, though it would be best of all to liken us to homesteaders. For we must live in the land that we seek out, and it will be in large measure what we make of it. Our involvement in the search is deep. We shall not one day return home as the explorer may expect to do. As we discover, so we live. All that is ours is what we discover, and no more. Our investment in our search is in which we are engaged, when the stake becomes our life itself.

> Our home is what we find and we are homesteaders with each moment a step into the unformed future,

living as we move in a home of our own making. It is this role that man has been cast and it does not seem to us that his nature is designed for any other, nor does it seem to us that the universe offers any other. We seek to make a home in this universe and it is our work. Our freedom lets us search. Our search is creating. Our creating is a finding – the fullest life that we can make our own.

Clark's *finding* and *freedom* were differed from the expression of faith in Judeo-Christian traditions. Thus in his 1951 sermon *Unitarianism – A Complete Religion?* he casts doubt on the need for any beliefs or a church:

In the fall when I discussed the four Christian conceptions of religion I had the incidental purpose of indicating that religion has more than one side to its nature. To be sure religion can be conceived in four different ways – more, of course – yet the different ways of conceiving religion must represent aspects of the same thing or perhaps emphases...

Almost no religion has been without...three aspects of [religion], belief, experience and church. A casual running through the catalogue of my piecemeal memory of both the great religions and primitive religions suggests that belief has been the most absent of the three. Primitive religion bothered little over beliefs. In the close community of the tribe a person settled into a routine of many daily and seasonal observances; no difference of opinion was ever suggested and the articulated beliefs were so meager as to amount to nothing. The attitude has prevailed until quite modern times when beliefs have emerged as worthy of attention. The great religions have incorporated a set of beliefs which grew in defiance of the established religion of the land for the difference must then be expressed in words. Confucianism is somewhat different for it has emphasized beliefs and never formed anything comparable to a church, but, of course, it did not offer a heavenly salvation in exchange for believing the right thing – it took modern Protestant Christianity to develop that notion...

Unitarianism suggests that the three should be used and how equal it is the task of making an adequate blending. Unitarianism has emphasized belief and experience while it has made the church secondary. It has also joined these first two with the opinion that one's belief should arise out of a man's own experience and should be a culmination of his own seeking. In this Unitarianism derives from Protestantism but even more from the thought of the last century that began to make feeling the central matter in religion and from the psychologizing of this century that set about examining man's inner life.

...At first glance Unitarianism holds then that a man's beliefs must come out of his own living experience and maintains only that no institution should dictate his beliefs but that it would be injurious for it to do so, what then is the place of the church? It would seem at best to tag along. And in Unitarianism I fear this has been the case. When it has been the traditional task of the church to provide beliefs and instruct man as to what his personal experience should be, it then becomes most difficult to understand the new role of the church when it must take a subsidiary place. Is the church needed at all? We can only point to the fact that Unitarianism has still maintained its churches at considerable cost of time and effort and money.

In spite of his somewhat tongue in cheek condemnation of religious requisites, Clark was the driving force in the expansion of Unitarianism in Saint Louis. He recognized that the denomination needed to grow and actively preached to make that possible. In

1953, five West Saint Louis County couples from First Church started a twice monthly Sunday afternoon family forum at a YMCA and were surprised when thirty-five enthusiastic people showed up for the first session. They decided to hold Sunday services as well, and Clark agreed to preach an early sermon, rushing back to First Church for its regular service. The group met in a dance studio in a Saint Louis suburb, and in 1955 they adopted the name Eliot Chapel and called Reverend John Fordon as their minister. In 1956, the Chapel moved to a rented house, but Fordon stayed only one year. In 1957, Martin Greenman was called, and land for a church was purchased in the northwest Kirkwood suburb. First Church generosity made this possible and Clark not only made the appeal for funds but continued, when necessary, to make a hurried trip to preach there. In 1959, Eliot Chapel voted to become independent of First Church and one year later called Webster Kitchell as the first permanent minister. In 1961, Grace Episcopal Church sold its historic building to the Chapel for $25,000, the value of the land. It has retained its name to this day and is now a thriving Unitarian church.

When Clark retired in 1969, First Church called William DeWolfe as its minister. The quality of preaching worsened dramatically to the dismay of many in the congregation. In his sermon on religious education called The Mediator-Catalyst, DeWolfe said:

> Our children come to us as a gift from Life. As Gibran suggests, we care for them, yet we can never own them. They belong to the future. The place is the First Unitarian Church, with a quality uniquely ours. We cherish the accumulated fields of human knowledge. We approach whatever we study with a sense of awe and reverence. We are committed to the freedom of the individual to search for his own meaning, to tolerance of different points of view, and to the use of reason. Ours is the responsibility to share with our children and youth in this approach which is the bedrock of our faith.

He could not match intellectually the scholarship of Clark and after three years the congregation asked him to resign.

In 1974 Earl Holt, a Starr King graduate, was called to the pulpit and remained at First Church for twenty-seven years. He had been assistant minister at the Plandome Unitarian Church on Long Island, New York, where he served two years. Thus he became the youngest minister to take the First Church pulpit and one with a distinct deist theology, a decided change from the Humanism of Clark. Holt believed in prayer; Clark never did. Holt believed that faith was important and he was convinced that Unitarianism required a strong faith to remain viable. Clark, if he used the word at all, applied it to the whole world and humanity. Holt's theology was demonstrated in 1991 when, after seventeen years in the pulpit, he preached four sermons on faith. Called *Sources of our Faith*, in the non-creedal Unitarian environment they came close to defining a doctrinal deism. Their message was an important contribution to Unitarian thinking. For Holt, faith was a necessary component for understanding the religion and was a vital element in its spiritual life. Holt started by explaining that talking about faith is not easy in the denomination:

> Ours is a church in which people believe a wide variety of different things. If you know nothing about Unitarianism, this is the one thing you are likely to know. So precious and central is this value of individual freedom of belief that we must regularly be reminded that it does not stand alone. I cringe whenever it is said that this is a church in which "you can believe anything you want" or where "you don't need to believe in anything". The first statement suggests religious anarchy, the second religious vacuity – both are negative statements, and both are simply untrue.
>
> A couple of weeks ago here I quoted the question of the Old Testament Amos, "Can two walk together unless they are agreed?" and suggested that even the smallest community cannot be formed unless its members be agreed on something, and something

substantial. We Unitarians have tended to make this such an icon of creedlessness that we tend to neglect or ignore the substantial things we have in common, and what I hope to show during the next few weeks is a series of sermons focusing on the common and unifying themes of Unitarian theology. What I shall attempt is quite paradoxical; doctrinal sermons in a non-doctrinal church. Whether this is possible we shall see.

He then started with the Bible and explained that it was at the center of Protestantism and also important to the early American Unitarians. Channing's famous Baltimore sermon was fundamentally a treatise on the biblical nature of Jesus. According to Holt, Channing considered the Bible "a book written for men, in the language of men, and its meaning is to be sought in the same manner as that of other books." Unitarians differ on how they regard the Bible. Unitarian Christians view it as essential but not authoritative. Humanists treat it as important literature with no particular religious significance. Holt went on to say:

The Bible is important because it is the primary source of the myths we are living now. Its stories are our stories even if we do not recognize them as such. They are our stories at unconscious and emotional levels which almost no other stories can reach. Whether we know them or not we are immersed in them, as they are reflected in both high and popular culture, in our art, our music and literature and much else besides…Unitarians remain a people of the book, even though it is not our only book, even though we feel free to be critical of it, even though we reject its claim to religious authority. Why? Simply because one cannot grow either as an individual or as a community by cutting oneself off from one's roots and heritage any more than one can grow on the other hand by blind acceptance and adherence to the words and ways of the past.

His next source of faith was identified as *Our Heritage and Hope*. It came at the height of public furor about the Clarence Thomas confirmation hearings involving Anita Hill, and Holt was certainly distracted by them. Drawing on the nation's Puritan heritage, he spoke of a Unitarian heritage shaped by a historical preoccupation with sexuality, ranging from Hawthorne's *The Scarlet Letter* to J. Edgar Hoover's collection of files. Holt then reverted to preaching in an almost conservative Christian style to remind the congregation that Unitarians had generally an earnestness that caused them "not to think they were saints, but they did not think it was foolish to try to be [one]." As he explained:

> Morality cannot be legislated, but goodness can be communicated…It is not enough to have the wisdom written in books, one needs the example of lived lives. That is what a church is for: to transmit the wisdom of experience from one to another and from generation to generation. This is a high purpose to which we often fail, even as we know we have failed as individuals, fail to even live up to the standard we set for ourselves. That is why there is forgiveness which requires the humility to recognize our errors and turn in the direction we should go. This kind of forgiveness is the source of hope, hope because we can begin again, hope because life does grant second chances, and hope because we possess a faith in the human capacity for renewal.

Holt's third sermon on faith covered *The Spirit*. More than the two previous sermons it revealed his distinct belief in the higher power that guides human action. It also demonstrated a sense of humor: "The classic Unitarian parable is a person who comes to a crossroad with signs labeled: 'To Heaven' and 'To a discussion group about Heaven.' The Unitarian, it is said, unhesitatingly chooses the latter path." Holt believed that any service must include a period of silence so that one can discern God, who speaks in a small voice. "If it seems that God is not speaking to us, it is very likely because we aren't giving Her (sic) a chance to get a word in edgewise." Holt then recalled the transcendental message of Emerson and Parker:

The ultimate source of religion was not in a church or in a book, but in the individual human soul. Revelation was not sealed, it did not end with the writing of the Bible, nor will it ever end. God speaketh, not spake, he [Emerson] said. If God revealed himself to the writers of the old testament and the new, so he might speak through anyone similarly dedicated and devoted to the life of the spirit. Jesus was not the unique miracle man of history but the symbol and emblem of the divinity which existed potentially in every human soul, which only needed awakening to recognize its own reality and greatness. And if God spoke through the prophets of Israel of old, God also spoke – and speaks – through other lands in other tongues. God spoke – and speaks – through the Hindu and the Buddhist and Zoroastrian as well as through the Jew and the Christian.

Moving to Parker and his great work on the *Transient and the Permanent in Religion* he remarked:

All religions are transient but religion is permanent because it grows out of something essential to the human soul. No particular religion itself is immortal. It is the pathos of the life of faith that it is in continual need of renewal, both in individuals and in institutions, because we are always clinging to the words and ways of the past. The word spirit means literally, breath. It is like a breath of wind, of air; it is here and it is gone…It is the central intuition of religion that in our little life we are breathing the larger life of God, one of whose names is Spirit.

Holt then defined what he believed religion to be:

…Religion stands for the perspective that there is something that stands above and outside and indeed against the things of the world, in judgment and perspective. It is the missing dimension in much of modern life, and many modern lives. It is what we refer to when we speak of being in but not of the world. It is realm of the spirit. Every day we make decisions that reveal what has the highest priority in our lives. Every day we decide what gods we will serve. Every day makes a claim on our lives, on our mind and heart and soul. Every day we make decisions based on what we believe, what we love, and what we truly live by. Therefore, every day is a day of judgment, and every day may be a day of revelation…The spirit that reveals itself in ordinary moments and speaks to us in the language of every day experience may be a profound source of our faith. All we need are eyes to see and ears to hear.

The last element of faith was the *Free Mind*, and this sermon summarized in many ways what Unitarians mean by freedom of beliefs. Holt maintained that faith is a story of rebellion against beliefs and against ideas one has spiritually outgrown. The Old Testament, according to Holt, is witness to this rebellion in the first chapters of Genesis when Eve courageously eats of the apple and gives it to man "and they knew." With this knowledge, however, also came fear, and it was at that point that humans became insecure, an insecurity that persists to this day. Holt went on to say that throughout American history, there have been displays of the free mind, starting with the founding fathers. But there was also doubt as to the success of the young republic and its concept of individual liberty. Holt cited Jefferson's statement, "I have sworn upon the altar of God, eternal vigilance against every form of tyranny over the mind of man." He also used the words of the Declaration of Independence in which liberty is included as an inalienable right granted to all by God. Holt concluded:

…the free mind is…not simply to doubt and to rebel, but to be freed for something higher and better. And this leads us to the problem of freedom in our own time, which is not the problem of escape, but the problem of what to do with the freedom we already possess, not to obtain freedom but to use it, not freedom from but freedom for…It is a counter-rebellion against the felt loss of established boundaries and certain answers, a longing for the comforts of boundaries and security. I understand the appeal and the impulse that lies beneath it, but ultimately I think there can be no real faith except that which nurtures the free mind, because doubt and rebellion are intrinsic to the free spirit.

In his long tenure at First Unitarian Church in Saint Louis, Holt was also active in furthering the growth of Unitarianism in the far western reaches of Saint Louis County. Two fellowships were established under his ministry. One failed but the other, with the financial support of First Church, would survive to become the Emerson Unitarian Universalist Chapel, establishing a fulltime minister in 1981. In 2001 Holt was called to King's Chapel in Boston and is currently its senior minister. He was succeeded at First Unitarian Church by Suzanne Meyer with a theology more akin to Parker's absolute religion. Her theology is described in chapter four.

CHAPTER 4:

The Modern Unitarian Faith

Unitarianism as a religious home for Americans has grown slowly in the last hundred years. The denomination merged with the Universalists in 1960 and the Unitarian Universalist Association (UUA) was formed one year later. The number of societies increased by ten in the period 1995 to 2007 and is steady at just over a thousand congregations. Membership has risen at less than one percent per year, statistically insignificant. Demographically Unitarians are predominantly white, college educated and relatively affluent. Politically they could be classed as liberal. A remarkable characteristic of modern United States churches is that of sixteen major congregations with a significant history in Unitarianism, eleven have women senior ministers. Members often join because they want their children to receive a Sunday school experience untainted by religious indoctrination. Thus in 2007 approximately 160,000 adults were 'certified members' of Unitarian congregations with about 60,000 children enrolled in church schools. On the surface the membership numbers can appear alarming; however they are comparable when compared to overall United States church attendance over the same period. In 1991 to 2004 church attendance in all denominations fell from 49 percent to 43 percent.[179] But when one applies other metrics to Unitarianism the denomination does not fare so well. Important politicians no longer join. There has been only one Unitarian president in the 20th century, William Howard Taft (1909–1913), and few prominent senators or congressmen since A. Powell Davis' ministry at All Souls Unitarian Church of Washington, D.C. during the mid-twentieth century. Prominent business leaders are generally not Unitarians. On the other hand professional people such as doctors, teachers, lawyers, and civil servants abound. Harvard Divinity School has been supplanted as a major source of Unitarian ministerial training by Meadville Theological School in Chicago and Starr King School for the Ministry in California. Few of these ministers started their life as Unitarians and many came from other professions.

The state of the Unitarian Universalist movement was described in a book by Michael Durell titled *The Almost Church: Redefining Unitarian Universalism for a New Era*. He was quoted in a recent sermon by Sharon Tomalin of the First Unitarian Church in Philadelphia:

> Durall writes that The Unitarian Universalist church as we know it is dying, and probably within the next 25 years. He cites some very convincing demographic trends to support his claim. There has been a mass exodus from mainstream Protestant congregations since the late 1950's. Further, it is estimated by numerous church observers that within a few decades, a least one third of the churches in the United States will close their doors. More specifically, Durall believes that four to five hundred of the slightly over one thousand UU churches will disappear. He observes that only about five percent of all congregations in the UU Association have seen measurable growth in the past decade. Of the 95% that have not grown, membership has plateaued or declined, their congregants have grow older and grayer, and pledge campaigns have typically fallen short of goals. Growth within the Association as a whole in the past decade has been about .8 percent. This is not eight percent; it is eight-tenths of one

percent. Many UU churches will close simply because they will not have the money to continue.

Tomalin then comments:

> Durall believes successful churches [have] their firm stand on dogma. Church members know what they are expected to believe, or they move on. Now, he doesn't expect us to suddenly become adherents of one particular set of religious beliefs, but we often define our faith so vaguely that it requires no mental, spiritual, or emotional commitment. For example, what does it mean, "to respect the inherent worth and dignity of every person" if it morphs into a worship of individualism so restrictive that it prevents us asking our members to contribute to the wellbeing of everyone? And prevents us expecting them to sacrifice time and money to sustain the church within and without its walls? And convinces us that the opinions and views of a relatively inactive person in our community, must somehow be accommodated to and given the same weight as those who attend and sustain the church more strenuously? Or caves in to, however active, those people who demand that their priorities be accommodated, or they will pick up their ball and go home? We try to be too much to too many. We need to narrow our focus and widen our outlook.

It is precisely this phenomenon that is implied in the title of this work *Faith under Siege,* though Durell's assessment seems to be more pessimistic than that of most members of modern Unitarian churches. Yet the very concept of God is questioned by the national organization, invoked by some ministers as a reality and discarded by humanists. The almost reflexive response of some Unitarians to the challenge of what they believe is that they cannot define it, that it might be God, and, by admitting that they really cannot understand what God really is, don't want to spend much time discussing it.

Thaddeus Clark, the long time and beloved minister of the First

Unitarian Church of Saint Louis, frequently reflected these doubts. In his 1958 Berry Street lecture is titled *Unitarianism Reincarnate* and is a review of the denomination's history with a high degree of skepticism. Regarding Jesus he refers to Albert Schweitzer:

> The timely is not held to be important. In fact, it does not have a good reputation. The timely is transient and therefore short lived. Religious things are expected to be more enduring, if not everlasting. This was the conclusion to *The Quest for the Historical Jesus* that was devastating. Schweitzer declared that Jesus belonged to his own time, and that our historical researches failed to capture him and bring him into our time. They did the reverse: they settled Jesus firmly in his own time. Jesus, in other words was supremely and exclusively timely.

> It is a question whether Schweitzer advanced or retarded liberal religion by this declaration. The interest of the liberals in Jesus grew out of their eagerness to discover him to be a moral leader and teacher, and their interest was keen. The traditional interest had little stake in his morals or the details of his life and was concerned only with his being a God who could confer a life after death upon the supplicant. The modern tradition of religious liberalism sought to bring Jesus into its world and make him a guide to the saving of this world if not its savior... Schweitzer's significance rested in his extensive review of New Testament scholarship, which he concluded by stating that Jesus' moral teachings could not be separated from Jesus' expectation that the world would come to an end within the lifetime of his companions. Therefore, his moral teachings could be expected to be applied only to his time that brief time – and not to all time. Much of New Testament scholarship since has been an attempt to find some way around Schweitzer's conclusion, some

reinterpretation, some historiographic device, that would reclaim Jesus from his own time and make him available for our time.

It was not just this one point in which Schweitzer found Jesus conditioned exactly by his own time and with appropriate words for his own time. Indeed, it was his whole message and his whole life, which was world-denying. Ever deeper study of the life of Jesus indicated at every point how involved he was in his own time, its tensions, its frustrations, and its turmoil. He died finally in his own time, for his own time, and at the hands of his own time. Thus he cannot be lifted up from this time past and set down in our own time. The question of what judgment Jesus would pronounce on this or that deed in this time is always irrelevant and unanswerable. He spoke for his own time. The implication, of course, is that this is a fault —at least a misfortune, perhaps even a deficiency – in the leader of Christianity. He should have spoken for all time and thus for our time. He should have spoken universal truths, but instead he was aggravatingly specific, and said to render unto Caesar – and the neighbor to be loved is the Samaritan.

And is this not what one finds when he turns back to the synoptic Gospels to read of Jesus? He finds a real person. He finds a man who was timely, who spoke to his own time, felt deeply with it, and would give himself for it. However much these accounts may be hearsay, and however much they may be legend, the person revealed is a real person. Real not merely in being an historical as opposed to a fictional figure, but real in being human, alive, fresh, warm, concerned, eager, involved, imperiled, suffering, loving, losing, and dying. If he were not of his own time and for his own time, he would not be all these things. And is this not what we prize and what we seek? The revelation of personal reality? His very value lies in that he was timely and because timely he was real and fully alive.

Clark, with his tendency towards Humanism, easily accepted Schweitzer's conclusion that Jesus had meaning only during his life time without describing his relevance today. Indeed throughout his ministry he analyzed religious and secular issues, raising questions but seldom providing definitive answers. These were the 1960 and 70s, and while the country debated social issues of rampant crime and poverty and how to alleviate these, Clark was observing:

> … these are only the beginnings of the doubts about the nature of the real person. Dare we treat people in the courts as if they were merely the products of their unhappy neighborhoods, whether the slums or an over-indulgent suburbia? Are people not something in themselves and to be held accountable for their own actions? We waver today between the notion that a man is not at fault for what he is because someone else has made him that, his neighborhood, the war, his companions, or his parents, and the notion that he must be taught forcefully what he failed to learn –which comes to look like mere vindictiveness. We wonder where the real person is in all this.

> A not greatly different puzzle arises over rehabilitation, one of the most popular of recent efforts at man's betterment. When we rehabilitate a man, whether from crime, mental illness, physical handicap, age, or mere lack of privilege, do we do more than find some adjustment for him? Some mode of life acceptable to the community where he must live? Some role for him to play out that is not unbecoming? Again we ponder over such a threat to the person as certain efforts for his welfare that are alleged to pauperize him. To pauperize a man is to make it profitable for him to become a pauper, I suppose, and no one

can any longer doubt that this has been the effect of some of our public welfare efforts. The role has been described quite vividly many times of families that have made a very happy adjustment to the relief check and the welfare lady.

These musings would be highly unpopular in today's Unitarian movement. They were a negation of every major social initiative of Unitarian ministers through the centuries to help the poor and support the weak, and they really are a remarkable statement by a minister who prided himself as educator and philosopher.

A lack of social compassion is seldom tolerated in today's Unitarian churches, while disdain for religion or the concept of a god will be condoned and does not disqualify a person from the ministry. As an example, Dr. John Wolf, at the time minister the of All Souls Church of Tulsa, expressed that feeling in his 1986 Berry Street Lecture titled *Religion, the Church and Our Mission in the World*. It counters many aspects of Unitarian history and tradition. He states:

> I have a theory that religion is the enemy. I have always been fascinated by it, and must freely admit that I have enjoyed studying it and discussing it. But I don't like it and I don't trust it. I don't like what it does to people. On the other hand, I love churches. I love them so much that it distresses me greatly when they get too involved with religion.

> Paul Tillich may have been of a similar mind when he spoke of the yoke of religion. Religion, he said, is a human invention, the natural result of the human predicament. We are finite beings. From dust we came and to dust we shall return. In the meantime, we are alive, and our lives imply something more than dust, something higher than our lowly natures, something grand. Else, we ask ourselves, why should we be here at all? Religion, said Tillich, is our great attempt to overcome our "anxiety and restlessness and despair, to close the gap within ourselves, and to reach

immortality, spirituality and perfection."... Except that, human as we are, all too soon we make a religion of our irreligion, and are caught again in our own toils. Or, (says Tillich) we find "new yokes outside the church, new doctrinal laws under which (we) begin to labor: political ideologies which (we) propagate with religious fanaticism; scientific theories which (we) defend with religious dogmatism; and utopian expectations which (we) pronounce as the condition of salvation for the world, forcing whole nations under the yoke of their creeds which are religions, even while they pretend to destroy religion.

Reason, freedom and tolerance are by no means the exclusive hallmarks of Unitarian Universalists. Indeed, as often as not, quite the contrary. In any case, they do poorly as articles of faith, or as philosophical constructs, for they too are fruit of the spirit, the products of a tortuous journey... Perhaps Unitarian Universalists have so few theologians for that reason: we are pilgrims, not apologists. We understand what it truly means to have lost our faith, to have experienced that exile when there seems to be no meaning, no purpose for our lives, when all those things that we are taught to believe no longer sustain us. Thence, we also know what it means to find another way, and when freedom means when we are no longer tied to those things we were told we had to believe, and how excellent it is to find others who would encourage and accompany us, and, finally, with their help, to discover how rewarding it is to learn to think for ourselves, to trust and to discover anew.

The message, it seems, is that the denomination needs leaders who can provide an alternate truth. Theology and faith have been supplanted by a constant search for this elusive truth, a truth that can take the place of past traditional beliefs but must be constantly rediscovered.

Yet faith is very much present in the life of today's All Souls Unitarian Church of Tulsa. It is not a conventional faith and almost impossible to place into a convenient bin of theist, Christian Unitarian or humanist theology. The church is a motivating force, not only when compared to other Unitarian churches, but also in terms of its role in the life of Tulsa and the denomination. With an adult membership in excess of fifteen hundred it is a leader in solving social concerns of the community and deeply involved in ecumenical affairs. Reviewing modern sermons by their minister, Marlin Lavanhar, reveals his deep commitment to and faith in the spiritual life of the people and community with no specific theological bias. Most revealing is his sermon *What in the Name of God are we Doing?* He talks about the mystery of our very existence, asserting that, as far as we know, we are the only intelligent life in the universe. He then asks his listeners to honor the miraculous nature of life on earth and all of the hundreds of generations that have come before. He highlights the historic role of the Tulsa church in the spiritual life of the community, particularly its 1965 it hosting of the first interfaith and interracial service. Lavanhar highlights the resurrection of the spirit as a new way of being religious: "As Unitarians we are building our cathedral to God and the human spirit and reject a religion that is all about saving souls in the next life. We are working to create the kingdom of heaven right here on earth". Levanhar thus has created a positive expression of faith in the human spirit to make a difference in the life of his church and in its community, a model perhaps, for the whole denomination. More importantly he has established a theme-based service format. It is shown in the monthly publication of the church called *Simple Gifts*. For the 2007 church year, monthly themes provided a theological insight into the broad aspects of Unitarianism. As Levanhar describes it:

> Congregants are offered multiple ways to engage the themes through worship, classes, branches groups, newsletter articles, at home practices for individuals and families, and a reading list. The resources are provided so that each person can decide how deeply to engage a particular theme. Children maintain

journals on the themes so they will have a record of their own theological understanding at various stages of their personal, spiritual and cognitive development. The themes offer the congregation (across the generations) a common set of stories, ideas, and topics to converse about each month. The story each month is usually Bible based, but occasionally the lead story is about famous Unitarians and Universalists. Each month, stories from other cultures and religions are used to demonstrate how similar topics are dealt with in other traditions. Members are given the opportunity to increase their Biblical literacy and to develop a theology informed by many faiths and rooted in Unitarian Universalism.[180]

Themes for the year included discussions about Creation, Democracy, God, Evil, Religious Authority, and Redemption. Thus All Souls may not have a set theology but it is able to express clearly both the spiritual and the religious aspect of worship. In the process it has created a congregation that truly understands the meaning of being Unitarian.

It may not be well known in the United States, but Unitarianism is a world religion. British Unitarianism is in decline and United States Unitarians exhibit a remarkable degree of parochialism towards international congregations. As described in chapter two, the American Unitarian Association had recognized the need to include foreign liberal religions. More recently, in 1995, that determination flagged, and the UUA voted against admission of foreign members. The result was that the International Council of Unitarians and Universalists (ICUU) is relatively unknown by congregations in the United States. In the ICUU publication titled *The Garden of Unitarian Universalism,* the origin of the organization and its philosophy is vividly described:

> In 1988, David Usher, a young Unitarian minister in England, proposed to the British General Assembly that a "World Unitarian Council" be established. The motion was passed unanimously, and … a meeting of Unitarians was held to discuss it. It had support from

some groups, including Canadians, but the largest (and wealthiest) group represented there, the UUA, was opposed. Six years and a new president later, the Unitarian Universalist Association (UUA) of the United States sanctioned the idea. An international committee was formed to plan and carry out an inaugural meeting in 1995 and the International Council of Unitarians and Universalists had set roots!

The full member groups range in size from the United States with around 160,000 members and over a thousand congregations to Finland with one lay-led congregation of twenty-two people. Some Unitarian and Universalist traditions are quite old; others are just taking root. Transylvanian Unitarians can trace their roots back to 1568 while the newest provisional member, Spain, was organized in 2000. The theology, practices, history and organizational structures vary around the world. In Lagos, Nigeria, the Unitarian Brotherhood Church, established in 1919, conducted services in the Yoruba language, and used native drums in their services. In Hungary and Transylvania, elected Bishops head the church and Unitarians there describe themselves firmly as Christian. In Germany, Deutsche Unitarier Religionsgemeinschaft was re-established in 1950 as a deliberately lay-led movement with a strongly humanist theology. The European Unitarian Universalists are actually several lay-led groups that meet annually in a retreat setting. In the Philippines, faith healing is an important part of the religious practice.

The group experienced some difficulties in arriving at a common statement of purposes, demonstrating the diversity of international Unitarians beliefs:

> ...in the first draft, the statement did not include the phrase 'to serve the Infinite Spirit of Life and the human community.' Arpad Szabo from Transylvania stated: "I can't go back to my people with a purpose that doesn't include 'to serve God.'" And Lene Shoemaker from Denmark responded, "I can't go back to my humanist congregation with a statement that does include it!" The group brainstormed for a wording that would satisfy all. When the phrase 'the Infinite Spirit of Life' emerged, Arpad was asked: "Would *the Infinite Spirit of Life* work for you?" Arpad answered with a smile, "Yes - but of course you know I will translate it as *God*".

The question and naming of a deity or life force that is involved in universal life has always been perplexing to Unitarians. As mentioned in the introduction, British churches had no such problem and include the word *God* in their statement of beliefs while openly expressing their desire to worship the divine. Their liberal philosophy is best expressed in the following comment regarding communion from their booklet: "Communion, where practiced [in Unitarian churches], expresses a simple sharing and fellowship our thanks for us and all great souls, solidarity with the cause of human welfare and recognition of the earth's bounty." Communion still exists in British Unitarian churches (as in some United States congregations).

In 1928, British Unitarians formed their current organization called the General Assembly of Unitarian and Free Christian Churches and in the early twentieth century the denomination was in a period of growth. Prominent people were proud of their identification with Unitarianism, including politicians, artists, writers, and professionals. Staring around 1950, however, there came a decline in membership that in 2008 has reached a low point of about 5,000 professed Unitarians in 182 churches and chapels, with another thirty-three congregations in Northern Ireland called the Non-Subscribing Presbyterian Church. At the 2008 annual meeting of the British General Assembly Reverend Art Lester, addressed this decline in his anniversary sermon by asking the question, "Why are we dying?"He answers this way:

It may be that we have stopped viewing God as someone you can really talk to. If that is so, then the happy-clappies have it all over us. Maybe God and the Spirit and all that have become nothing more than an idea, a topic for discussion. Maybe it means that we think that God isn't really there at all, that He has joined the mobs in the great drive-in temples of loony America, and left us to merely philosophize. And if God doesn't make an appearance in church on Sunday, how can we expect to see anyone who is actually looking for Him?

This comment starkly illustrates a problem that the world-wide denomination faces: some Unitarian ministers totally intellectualize religion and also Unitarian beliefs.

The very liberal avoidance of the deity holds even when there is an argument in the secular world about the theory of evolution; then Unitarians with a rare unanimity condemn any vestige of Creationism. They cite with great satisfaction the immense literature on cosmology, fossil evidence, gene theory, and natural selection. To almost every Unitarian Creationism or even Intelligent Design is pseudo-science, a vestige of a nineteenth century debate that has been adopted by today's religious fundamentalists to justify the biblical story of Genesis. Yet many accept as scientific truth the Big Bang theory whereby a tiny bit of undefined matter expanded into the universe with laws of physics that defy human imagination. Even a respected cosmologist like Stephen Hawkins postulates that there must have been a force before creation and that the precision of the Big Bang strongly suggest the existence of God. Other scientists marvel at evolution and accept a higher being. Most modern Unitarians thus justifiably reject the Hebrew god with beard and flowing robe and fewer accept prayer and a life force that can be called *God*. Most believe in a higher power but would rather not give it a name.

The diversity of beliefs within the Unitarian movement has broadened since its beginnings. Today's churches still range from Christian Unitarian to humanist, but all accept the *UUA's Statement of Principles* that recognize earth based religions. Sermons may be theist or a commentary on the modern scene; they can range from expressions of faith to political analysis. Meditations can be addressed to God, to a higher power or to nature, or they may be poetry or simple periods of silence. Hymns can be traditional and Christian or redacted to take out words of religion or those that are politically incorrect, i.e. God or gender. The standard holy days are celebrated with reverence or ambivalence, but very few ministers can escape the Christian origins of these festivals. If one wants to gauge the theology practiced in modern Unitarian churches across the country one can use two yardsticks. The first is simply what text is used in the doxology carried over from Christianity and used in many congregations. In those that are more theist, the text uses Charles Lyttle's words "Praise God the love we all may share, Praise God the beauty everywhere, Praise God the love of good to be, Praise God the truth that makes us free." More humanist inclined ministers prefer the modern Vincent Silliman version: "From all that dwell below the skies, Let songs of hope and faith arise, Let peace, good will on earth be sung, Through every land by every tongue."

The second is more complex, namely an analysis of sermons preached to test how they fit in the spectrum of Unitarian beliefs. Are they a development of religious faith or an appeal to reason alone, or do they deal with the soul or political orientation? The problem is that nowhere in the UUA's statement of principles is there a mention of faith. The contradiction is described in a sermon by Galen Guengrich, Senior Minister of All Soul's Unitarian Church in New York City. In a sermon titled The *Dangerous Edge of Things*, he tries to explain the constant conflict between religion and science, between reason and revelation, and inevitably he comes to the issue of faith. He says:

> ... how do we decide what to believe? If scientific knowledge comes from human reason, where does faith come from, if it is not human assent to supernatural revelation? Let me be candid here. Faith is something no one fully understands. It peers into the realm of mystery and transcendence, of meaning and purpose, of value and satisfaction. In the modern world, people of enlightened faith live on

the boundary between science and religion. For this reason, when we talk about faith, as the poet Robert Browning once said, "Our interest's on the dangerous edge of things. The honest thief, the tender murderer, the superstitious atheist." To which list we might add the skeptical believer. In my view, faith stands at the dangerous edge of things: on the boundary between things we know for certain and things we can never fully comprehend. This boundary can be violated in two ways... [Those] thoroughly religious can easily allow their faith to run roughshod over scientific knowledge. Antireligious people, on the other hand, can easily allow scientific certitude to drain life of the mysteries and satisfactions of faith.

From Guengrich, one can conclude that those who refuse to accept the unknowable and unseeable risk missing the power of faith that can make life more fulfilling. As Jesus to Thomas: "Have you believed because you have seen me? Blessed are those who have not seen me yet believe." There is so much in this world that we cannot see and yet accept on faith. Or as Guengrich concludes:

When we say that all people are created equal, for example, we are not saying that scientists have proven that every human being is equal in some objective sense. Rather, we are committing ourselves to live as if equality is a universal truth. When some element of our faith is proven false, however, it should be abandoned. When shown to be harmful to others, it should be reformed. When shown to be indifferent to the fate of the natural world, it should be rejected. Because faith stands at the dangerous edge of things, it is always at risk of either withering away or turning demonic. At its best, however, faith is a commitment to live as if certain things are true, and thereby help to make them so... Faith is a commitment to live as if life is a wondrous mystery, as if love is divine, as if life is good, as if we are responsible for the well-being of those around us. Faith is a commitment to live fervently and devoutly, with eyes wide open and mind fully engaged, but also with heart open to mystery and soul attuned to the transcendent. My point is that people of enlightened faith must attend carefully to the difference between mystery and magic. Supernatural religion has everything to fear when confronted by the purifying fire of reason, but faith has everything to gain. Once the dross of magic has been skimmed away, people of enlightened faith no longer need to be tentative or half-hearted. They can give themselves fully to their faith—as if it is true.

In effect, he is adapting Parker to modern times, discarding the transient and retaining the permanent.

John Buehrens, past president of the UUA, does believe that Unitarians are a community of faith, In a sermon he preached at the First Unitarian Church of Philadelphia he maintained that Unitarians have *A Progressive Faith From the Inside Out*. In his words:

… some people want to build the human future on the basis of narrow, exclusive enclaves of cultural and religious identity. They want to turn the meaning of kinship – the ancient spiritual wisdom, taught in every tradition, that we are all sisters and brothers –inward on itself. Our mission, yours and mine, is to capture the inner core of the universal spirit of religion at our inner core. And then to work with other people of progressive religious spirit to re-unite that sense of kinship to every society's effort to re-unite spiritual freedom with greater equality of opportunity. For there is no solution to be found just in secular consumerism or nostalgic and oppressive patterns of belief. The only solution is to be found in communities and people willing to reach out from the inside, toward the humanness in people of other backgrounds, toward concern for their rights, dignity, democratic aspirations, and our common future.

Never doubt, then, that we have a mission in this church. To paraphrase one of our great ministers of the last generation, it is to make religious people more progressive and to help progressive people live the religious spirit of doing justice, loving kindness, and walking humbly before that Mystery which transcends us all. To bring them the good news of a progressive form of faith lived from the inside out, not forced on anyone from the outside in. A form of faith in which we know that "belief is many things; and so is disbelief; but true religion is what happens to us when we open our minds to new truth, our hearts to greater compassion, and give ourselves to the service of justice.

In spite of his use of the term mystery when he mentions "a progressive form of faith" or talks about "religious people," when he defines Unitarian beliefs to be "many things," true faith may be hard to find.

If the concept of faith is muted in the UUA's statement of principles, the UUA's admonition to accept Earth-centered traditions is highlighted as a sign of diversity in theology. It is unclear, however, what audience is addressed with the phrase: "Spiritual teachings of Earth-centered traditions which celebrate the sacred circle of life and instruct us to live in harmony with the rhythms of nature." The first thing that comes to mind is Buddhism which describes life as an ever closed circle. Thubten Chodron defines it as follows: "Each moment of mind is a continuation of the previous moment. Who we are and what we think and feel depends on who we were yesterday. Our present mind is a continuation of yesterday's mind. This continuity can be traced back to our childhood and to being a fetus in our mother's womb. Even before the time of conception our mind stream existed. In previous moments we were linked to another body."[181] Buddhism has characteristics that presage Christianity. Supposedly a male child had planted itself in the womb of a queen: "And he, if he continues to live he will become a Universal Monarch, but if he leave the household life and retire from the world, he will become a Buddha, and roll back the clouds of sin and folly of this world."[182] There is also the concept of celibacy and rebirth, albeit in an ever continuing circle. Rebirth refers to a person's mind taking one body after another under the power of ignorance and contaminated actions. While we are alive, our body and mind are linked, but at death they separate. Each has its own continuum. The body becomes a corpse, and the mind continues on to take another body. Some of these life forms – hellish ones, hungry ghosts, and animals – experience more suffering than happiness. Other life forms- humans, demi-gods, and gods are considered relatively happy births. Beings repeatedly take rebirth in all of these life forms until they free themselves from ignorance and attain liberation.[183] If one takes a very broad view, this might have become the Christian story of sin determining the soul's eventual destination – heaven or hell. Buddha could be the redeemer like Jesus who is without sin.

Disconcerting for theist is the sudden appearance of pagans and wiccans as part of the Unitarian movement. Their inclusion in the UUA principles came about through the strong Unitarian feminist movement of the late 20th century that also brought about the cleansing of hymnals, prayers and sermons from gender specific words such as *God the Father* and *man* as a synonym for *human*.

What then is a Wiccan? The Encyclopedia Britannica has a description of the modern movement harkening back to its modern founder Gerald Brousseau Gardner:

> Despite variation within the Wiccan community, most believers share a general set of beliefs and practices. They believe in the Goddess, respect nature, and hold both polytheistic and pantheistic views. Most Wiccans accept the so-called Wiccan Rede, an ethical code that states "If it harm none, do what you will." Wiccans believe in meditation and participate in rituals throughout the year, celebrating the new and full moon, as well as the vernal equinox, summer solstice, and Halloween, which they call Samhain. Wiccan rites include invoking the aid of the deities, practicing ceremonial magic, and sharing a ritual meal.[184]

Wiccans supposedly are rebelling against the traditional

religions that are autocratic, paternalistic, sexist, homophobic, and insensitive to the environment, views that Unitarianism had rejected for decades. The inclusion of Wiccans poses the danger that the theology based on Judeo-Christian traditions and faith is diluted to the point where Unitarian identity is lost.

Despite the UUA's principles most ministers do have to deal with the reality of faith and the fact that modern Unitarian congregations are made up of many who believe in a god, even though they have trouble defining the term, as well as those who are agnostic and or atheist. Thus ministers often must address the definition of the word *God.* Suzanne Meyer, minister of the First Unitarian Church in Saint Louis addressed this in a sermon titled *What do you mean by God?* She maintains that many Unitarians answer this by saying that it depends on what is meant when one uses the term. To her the word and indeed the belief in a God is neither the beginning nor the end of the religious dialogue. Instead, she says that the religious experience includes the "deep sense of connection to all living things... the encounter with wonder, inspiration and transformation." She adds: "God is not a proposition to prove but a reality to experience; not something to define but to know in the mind's commitment to truth, in the claims of justice, in the prevalence of beauty and in the sanctities of love."

Laurel Hallman, Senior Minister of the First Unitarian Church of Dallas, discussed faith and God in her 2003 Berry Street lecture titled: *Images for Our Lives.* She believes the denomination is conflicted about the terms because they are metaphors for concepts that are hard to define:

> I want to talk about imagination. About *religious* imagination, to be more specific. I want to say that we are in a crisis of language, (and I believe that we are), because we have forgotten what religious imagination is and does. The purpose of my essay today will be to remind us of the importance of religious imagination in all our varied ministries. In ministry itself... Today I want to say that one of the reasons we are having a crisis of language among ourselves... is because we have been charmed, sometimes by the sound of

our own voices, sometimes by the brilliance of our own minds, speaking eloquently about this or that, but forgetting the foundation of our work in the world—the religious existential dimension of life. The communication from person to person and generation to generation of a kind of truth that is based on the reality--as Bernard Meland once said—it is a truth based on the reality "that we live more deeply than we think".

To her the words used in Unitarian churches are "Religious Imagination" and she goes on to define her own beliefs:

...and then I was to discover that the word, for example "God", could become the victim of what Whitehead called "Misplaced Concreteness". Words, over time, could lose their rich, metaphorical, living depth, and become concrete—rigidified and lifeless. The imaginative vitality could ebb away. The word "God" could die...So if words don't stand still; if they are subject, over time to misplaced concreteness; if they don't necessarily represent one theology or another; if they are inadequate, even when they serve political and psychological purposes, even when they give us some meaning and purpose; if words need to point to the depths of lived experience, (the religious existential dimension of life;) if we live more deeply than we can think; if we are currently in a crisis of language (which I believe we are;) if we are truly to minister in the fields of human need, what will save us from ourselves?

I recently spoke to our Adult Sunday School Class in Dallas on the topic "Why I am not a theist". They packed the room to hear what I had to say, because of course they thought I was. Why did they think I was a theist? Because I use the word God. Because I pray in the midst of the worship service. I was embarrassed a bit myself, to find that I had failed to make the distinction that the use of metaphors and poetry and scripture has to do with religious imagination, and not with one theological category or another.

Thus to Reverend Hallman, at least, the words of scripture have true meanings that are left to the imagination of ministers and churchgoers. The reality is that most Unitarians do have a faith based view of life but each person's definition of faith will differ.

In 2006 Reverend Jennifer O'Quill, minister of the Second Unitarian Church of Chicago, preached sermons that address this issue directly. Titled *Sources of Our Faith* they are probably some of the most concrete expressions of Unitarian theist beliefs. She claims that how we listen to others says a lot about who we are, and she asks what can be done to help a church community learn to give voice to faith and talk to one another about it. Indeed it is sometimes impossible even to find the words to express what the term means for a Unitarian Universalist. But she does find words and in the process draws on the emotions that many have missed in Unitarian worship. Her service format, mixing sermons with poetry and unabashedly sharing personal experience, and an obvious love of life, enables her love, faith and humanity to shine through and draw in her audience. Reverend O'Quill also ties some of these sermons to defining moments in the history of the Unitarian movement, starting with Servetus and the concept that for Unitarians God is One. Her imaginary conversation between Servetus and King Sigismund of Transylvania should be a Unitarian classic: "You know King, it is a simple idea: one God, one creative force at work in the world. I just think it is a lot more complicated for God to have all these parts. God in the flesh of Jesus Christ, God in the Holy Spirit and God as God's self. It simplifies things just to believe in one God."

O'Quill goes on to say that she believes in the historical Jesus and respects his teachings, but her faith also leads her to value prophets from other religions.[185] Next she turns to the God of love, basing her sermon on Universalism:

> Universalism bloomed as a faith that freed people of a God of fear and judgment, and ushered in a faith that said: God's Love is so vast, that it covers all people, all living creatures, the whole of creation. No

one can be beyond the reach of this holy Love, and this Love is revealed in all kinds of ways, through different peoples and faith. For the Universalists, Jesus Christ was so filled with this spirit of Love, that his life became filled with words and deeds that revealed his depth of faith and the great and amazing love of God. His life reveals to us how we too might incarnate that Divine Love in our own lives and reveal that Love with our own words and deeds.

She then defines God from the standpoint of direct experience. God is:

... the ability to feel connected to the whole of creation: when we are walking in the woods and suddenly feel ourselves as an integral part of the whole of creation; when we stand by the sea, or in front of our favorite painting with a sense of wonder and awe for its beauty, its power; when we hold our child in our arms, or fall into the arms of our lover, grateful for the love that seems to burst from our every cell in our body. All of this creates the religious impulse.

Lastly she tries to reconcile the religious component of faith with Humanism. She explains that Humanism is about saving the world of today. In fact she asserts that humanism's impact on our tradition has made the question of an afterlife non-essential. While not talking about an afterlife she ends by saying that she personally believes that, if there is in fact another place, one of the interview questions will be: "How well did you taking care of the last place you were in?"

Unitarian faith is also the topic of Forrest Church, Minister of Theology of All Soul's Church in New York City. He clearly defines what the term means for many Unitarians in his sermon *What I Believe*:

As the negative print image of every form of fundamentalism, Unitarian Universalism offers to the world an alternative religious vision. Rather than rend, we sew. We celebrate unity, twice in our very name. As for liberal, the world means "generous, flexible and free." And yet, this saving power, the power of our good news, will come alive only if we bring the same passion to our liberal faith—to our open-handed, open-hearted, open-minded faith—that others bring to theirs.

Religious experience springs from two primary sources, awe and humility. Neither awe nor humility is served by those who refuse to go beyond the letter—either of scripture or of science—to explore the spirit. Fundamentalists come in two basic varieties. Right-wing fundamentalists enshrine a tiny God on their altar. Fundamentalists of the left reject this tiny God, imagining that by so doing they have done something creative and important. Both groups are in thralldom to the same tiny God. Theology is poetry not science. During our brief span, we interpret the greatest and most mysterious masterpiece of them all, the creation itself. The creation is our book of revelation, not a bound book vouchsafed to us by some ancient guru. We rely on the oracle of our own experience, drawn from our reading of the book of nature and of human nature, including our reading of the Bible and our study of philosophy. The text of meaning is vast, its nuances many and various.

In what I call the Cathedral of the World there are millions of windows, each telling its own story of who we are, where we came from, where we are going, each illuminating life's meaning. In this respect, we are many. But we are also one, for the one Light shines through every window. No individual, however spiritually gifted, can see this Light—Truth or God, call it what you will—directly. We cannot look God in the eye any more than we can stare at the sun without going blind. This should counsel humility and mutual respect for those whose reflections on ultimate meaning differ from our own.

Gaze into the light of the heavens. There are 1.7 trillion stars for every living human being. The star to person ration is 1.7 trillion to one. That is awesome and it counsels humility. It should certainly discourage the scourge of human pride. But does it? No. Instead, we sit on this tiny, munificently fixtured rock arguing over who has the best insider information on the creator and the creation. Is it the Christian? The Buddhist? The Atheist? The Humanist? The Theist? Please! We humans trumpet our differences, even kill each other over them, while, in every way that matters, we are far more alike than we are different. We are born into the same mystery and the same sun sets on each of our horizons. The acknowledgement of essential unity is a central pillar of Unitarian Universalism. In contrast, fundamentalists, perceiving the Light shining through their own window, conclude that theirs is the only window through which it shines. They may even incite their followers to throw stones through other people's windows. Secular materialists make precisely the opposite mistake. Perceiving the bewildering variety of windows and worshippers, they conclude there is no Light. But the windows are not the Light; the windows are where the Light shines through.

This sermon is powerful and thought provoking. For Forrest Church faith is not under siege. Instead he believes it needs to be carefully explained to a population that is bombarded on all sides with religious messages that ignore the human spirit and human decision making.

The theist message of faith is also expressed in the 2005 Berry Street lecture by Burton D. Carley, minister of the First Unitarian Church of Memphis. He titled his address *The Way Home*. His thesis is that every human, Unitarians included, has an undefined longing for a path home, "out of the hollow to the hallowed," where the hallowed home, is God. He continues the metaphor:

> To go home we must come to terms with who we are as a people. We have demystified Christianity and yet there is a need to be able to talk about the Mystery in which we live and move and have our being. We have deconstructed the miracles out of the biblical narratives and yet the human heart still seeks a sense of the miraculous, a sense of eternal possibility that offers hope beyond human cunning. We have shorn superstition away from the body of spiritual wisdom and yet we are in need of linguistic tools for interpreting the deep yearnings and discoveries of our inner lives. Science cannot do this. Psychology cannot do this…We need symbols and narratives and the ferment of the poetic imagination to talk about the edges of human experience, to speak about the intersection between the temporal and the eternal, to express what is true beyond facts and to point to the Reality beyond the real.[186]

Carley thus seems to address directly the initial thesis of this book, that there is a crisis of faith in Unitarianism, and he provides a theological path to solve it by meeting the spiritual needs of every human being. He requires not a creed, but rather the emotional foundation for a religious experience based on our Christian tradition.

Reverend John Morehouse, minister of the Pacific Unitarian Church in Los Angeles, has a more humanist message of faith. He tries to address the question of a new member as to what a Unitarian faith is:

> Faith is a funny word. It means to believe with all your heart and your entire mind. It is that belief which gets you through the night. It's that belief that takes you to your death. When those firefighters ran back into the burning World Trade Center, they did so with faith, not a belief, not a position statement,

but with faith: faith that their destiny in life is to save lives even if they lose their life in the process. This is what it means to be faithful. Belief is provisional, faith is certain. By joining each Sunday we enter into not only a community of open-minded spiritual seekers but in an endeavor to build our faith. This isn't a social club or a debating society. This is a religion. We may all have our opinions but at the end of the day, when the long night stretches before us, when we want to know what to do or how to get on, we want faith.

He goes on to elaborate by postulating a number of principles,

We believe in each other. Our Gods are not the same, much less the same fortress. We believe many things about the ultimate nature of the cosmos but what is real is the help we can give each other.

We believe in pursuing justice. "Faith is the sister of justice" wrote the Unitarian theologian James Luther Adams. We are called by virtue of being human but especially as Unitarian Universalists.

We believe in good and evil. Let me start with evil. Regardless of where you think evil comes from; we have to believe evil exists. It is not merely the absence of good. It is a force unto itself. The perpetrators might not call themselves evil but the taking of innocent life is the worst manifestation of wrongful doing. Evil exists in our world. Accept that as a faith statement and face it squarely. We believe in good. Who here remembers the story about the Old Italian couple who planted new grape vines in a vineyard they would never see to fruition in the shadow of a coming war? The impetuous young man walks by and asks "Old man, why you plant what you will never taste the fruit of?" The old man smiles and says, "I plant because the good never dies."

Only at the end does he address the religious aspect of faith as the seventh principle:

> Finally, we believe in the mystery of God. None of us knows the ultimate answers to the ultimate question of why we are here and where we are going. We have certain faiths in the stories and that is good. But ultimately, as Moses was to learn, God is not to be seen. We can find metaphors to describe the ultimate being of which we are all apart but they are only maps to the territory, to the mystery that some of us would call God. The saying goes that the map is not the territory.

Indeed every Sunday is a challenge for the Unitarian minister since the congregation is diverse in belief but unified in a search for meaning. Forrest Church calls this search the most basic need for every human being. In a recent sermon titled *Mother God,* he stated that ninety-five percent of Americans feel they must build a relationship with God:

> Today, when people boast to me that they don't believe in God, I ask them to tell me a little about the God they don't believe in. Almost surely, I don't believe in "Him" either. It is easy to torch a straw God. Those who do so appear to believe that by destroying God the Father, Almighty Lord and King, Master and Judge of the Universe...they are pursuing religion itself to the grave.

In his sermon on theology he goes further:

> God is not even God's name. God is our name for a power that is greater than all and yet present in each: the life force; the Holy; Being itself. God doesn't exist only because we need God; we exist because the universe was pregnant with us when it was born...in my experience, only by positing the existence of a power beyond our comprehension can we begin to account for the miracle of being with an appropriate measure of humility and awe. I recognize

that for many people the word 'God' has shrunk from repeated use, but we can always re-stretch it. If you can't manage to do this—the 'G word' fitting your mind more like a straightjacket than a divine garment—simply substitute another. "Spirit" may work for you, or "the Sacred" or your 'Higher Power'. So long as the object of your reverence is large enough, it doesn't really matter, not at all.

These words would be acceptable to most Unitarians but not to a confirmed humanist. Thus Kendyl Gibbons, senior minister of the First Unitarian Society of Minneapolis, in her sermons seldom mentions God or faith. Much of her preaching is based on reason, and in her sermon on the Humanist Identity she provides an insight to her belief system:

We affirm our Humanism in the practices of freedom, reason and respect, both in our own personal behavior, and also in the principles that we support in our culture and society. Humanism begins with the surprisingly daring proposition that ordinary individuals are the best judges of what will make them happy, and that to a very great extent, people should be allowed to do whatever it is they think is most likely to make them happy. This freedom has limits, of course, where it impinges on the freedom or well being of others, but it teaches us in a fundamental way that as we do not wish for anyone else to impose their views on us for our own good, so we must not seek to impose our views where they are not shared. Side by side with our commitment to freedom stands our insistence upon the guiding power of reason. This is not to say that all our experiences, or even all our decisions, are perfectly rational. No human being has ever achieved such a state, and in some sense to do so would be to cast off the organic nature of our existence. We recognize that we are creatures of instinct and impulse, of needs and yearnings that are not always logical, and Humanism teaches us to be content with that reality, not to seek to transcend it into some realm of disembodied ideas and perfection.

The contrast could not be more distinct: it is between living by faith or by a set of ethics.

Dr. Edward Frost is Minister Emeritus of the Unitarian Universalist Congregation of Atlanta. He too had to grapple with the question of faith in the absence of either a Unitarian creed or belief in an afterlife. He bears witness to life-long Unitarians with critical illnesses turning to traditional Christianity in their final days to save their souls. In his sermon *A Faith for all Seasons* Frost tries to define what Unitarians mean by terms like *God* and *faith*:

> My faith -- the undergirding theology of my ministry--is that there is in the wholeness of the universe a power of Creativity -- God, if you will -- which is the continuing process which seeks to bring all things in existence to their fulfillment. The human task, and the task of religious community, is to create the social conditions, to create the world, and to create the kind of human relationships, through which that Creativity can transform us.
>
> Transformation is a continuing, open-ended *process*. Dogmatic beliefs, claims to have the only and the final truth, close the doors to process and discovery. No matter how comforting beliefs may be, when they are dogmatically held they bind us to one place and to one narrow view of existence. The transformation we seek in religious community is not mere personal salvation or personal assurance but the salvation, the transformation, the continuing re-creation of *all* humanity and *all* being. That all life, all being, is in continual re-creation and transformation is a faith -- faith being a choice of how to understand existence and our place in it... Ours is not a faith for another world. It is not a faith for other-worldliness. It is a faith for this world, this life, this moment as this moment moves into the next. It is a faith out

of which we commit to the transformation of our lives, of all lives, and of the way we live with each other and with the earth. It is a faith in which we are persuaded that this is the life we have to live, to create and re-create out of sorrow and loss, out of pain and frequent incomprehensible horror, and out of love and sublime joy.

One might surmise that Frost is theologically closer to the humanist belief in individual acts rather than to an acceptance of the divine. In fact he is troubled by the term *church* in Unitarian use and the concept that they are part of Christianity. In his sermon titled *Are Unitarians Christians or Not* he reveals his Humanism:

I feel quite comfortable in saying that this is not a Christian congregation. At the same time, it is not a Jewish congregation. It is not a Buddhist or Wicca or Islamic congregation. Our congregations exist in an era in which our ministers--even our youngest ministers--are trained in seminaries (a Christian term) which, while decidedly liberal in their perspective, are grounded still in the Protestant models of curriculum, worship forms, language and practice.

I was stripped of my traditional Christian faith in a liberal, Protestant seminary. But I was, nevertheless, sent into the world to minister with the institutional Christian church as the only model I knew and -- outside of a couple of courses in comparative religion-- with Christian theology the only theology I knew. And I am not untypical of the ministers of our congregations. Consequently, our worship forms remain essentially Protestant: we have hymns, prayers, offerings, and--what in seminary we called "the hymn sandwich"--the sermon between two hymns. There is some experimentation here and there but, for the most part, most ministers and congregations rest into the known and comfortable forms and categories.

> I've been avoiding the word "Church". Some
> Unitarian Universalists who do not have a Christian
> heritage, drawn into our congregations by the promise
> of diversity, hear terminology, such as "church," as
> belying the promise. Those who have experienced
> or who have been raised in the knowledge of the
> centuries of Christian abuse, terror and genocide, are
> offended by the words of the Christian lexicon--like
> "Church". I try to be sensitive to the sense of affront;
> but consider this, again in relation to the Protestant
> culture: the term "church," to most people simply
> refers to the place. Even in the congregation I once
> served which called itself The Unitarian Society,
> the people still spoke of going to the church. They
> wouldn't have known what else to say where they
> were going. The Society was the people, perhaps. But
> the building was a church

Frost thus presents an example of the importance many humanist Unitarians place on words that can be classed as religious.

Another reliable indicator of the theology of a Unitarian church is the format of the Christmas service and its Easter sermon, because these holidays directly challenge Unitarian beliefs regarding the Bible, Jesus Christ, and the Resurrection. In fact often one hears an introduction along these lines: "I am not sure what I should say about Easter but...". The 'but' is often based on Parker's 1841sermon on the *Transient and Permanent in Christianity* and is often followed by a differentiation between "the religion of Jesus and the religion about Jesus." When Kendyl Gibbons comes to Easter, the tone from the purely reasoned argument above is somewhat modified. Her sermon is titled *Easter NOT for Dummies* and is a cogent discussion not only of the biblical story of Jesus but also of the Unitarian view of Christianity harking back to Parker's sermon. She defines as permanent the religion *of* Jesus and as transient the religion *about* Jesus and then adds:

> If we are to criticize traditional interpretations
> of Christianity with any degree of credibility, we
> need to understand the historical realities and the

academic arguments that support our skepticism, as well as the sometimes surprising extent to which that skepticism is shared within the believing community. The cardboard caricature of Jesus that was offered to many mainline Protestants in the mid-twentieth century, especially to children, is one of the most ephemeral products of Christianity's transient dimension; it flattens and distorts the radical nature and power of its story. Yet this is the image by which many people- many Americans, anyway-evaluate the significance of the Christian message, and thereby underestimate both its appeal, and its relevance to the human condition.

The message is that thinking Unitarians must deal with the historical Jesus but not with his supposed sacrifice or sacrificial atonement that are fundamentally undocumented by his contemporaries.

Earl Holt, minister of Boston's King's Chapel, deals with the gospel accounts of Jesus' resurrection in a more reverent way. He mentions the four conflicting accounts of Mark, Matthew, Luke, and John and concludes that they agree in one respect; there was no doubt that the tomb was empty. Naturally, there was a lot of confusion but it was the women who first spread the Easter message and thus it is a story that two thousand years later has not yet come to an end. He then draws this conclusion:

> We commonly speak of Jesus' resurrection as if it were something that happened to him. And it is obviously true that something did happen to him in actual fact and time but what exactly happened is an unlockable mystery. The Resurrection story in its fullness, however, is not that only. It is about what happened to Jesus but it is also about what happened and has happened to countless others, in his time and through all time since. Individually as Christians we come to our own differing conclusions and understandings of what had happened on that first Easter, but what unites us as Christians is our common and ongoing

participation in that mystery which is the center of our faith, the Resurrection, the promise of a new life made by him who for us is the way, the truth and the life. Every Sunday is a Little Easter and once a year on this Big Easter we contemplate the mystery in which it began, in the seeming end that was really a beginning.

Peter Lanzillota, minister of the Charleston, South Carolina church maintains that the dominant and contrasting emotions of Easter were fear and joy, and he quotes the account of the resurrection in Matthew as his source:

> In this gospel account...the two Mary's greeted the news and the experience of that first Easter with the contrasting emotions of fear and joy, and who could blame them? They unexpectedly were confronted with a complete reversal – a gracious but seemingly unbelievable occurrence! What they heard, what they experienced was quite extraordinary! The event that became the first Easter was something that defied all their previous experience, and any rationally held cultural norms and beliefs.... According to both mystical and psychological typologies, fear is seen as the anchor point in the development of our egos, and therefore is regarded as a universal emotion, and acts as a frequent malady that often arises in any worldwide religious context.

> The archetypical image of a majestic angel at the tomb signifies the holiness and wholeness of the event; not as a literal factual even to be sure, but it symbolically acts to remind us of this supernal truth: that whatever we bury within the tomb of our fearful human awareness can and does endure; but fear can also resurrect and transform itself in faith; in hope, in love, and become a new real presence in our hearts.

Lanzellotta expressed the religious nature of the holiday and probably represents a Unitarianism much like that of Channing.

Carl Scovel, who preceded Earl Holt as minister of King's Chapel, has a similar view. He states:

> What is spirituality? ... As I hear the word being used, it speaks to me first of all of an individual yearning for and reaching for some experience and some conviction of that which is greater than self, yet fulfilling of self. I do not use the word "spirituality" to describe behavior patterns, such as lighting candles or a chalice, praying, meditating, sharing concerns. Spirituality, the yearning and reaching, may lead to behavior patterns, but I hear it used to describe the motive force for behavior. I hear it as the primal, inchoate, diffuse need, often indefinable at the onset.
>
> I called spirituality an individual yearning and groping. As you know, it is more than that. It is a movement. In the last decade we have seen in our country a growing interest in and desire for rituals, reading, retreats, workshops, disciplines, and conversations which enhance the life of the soul. We've seen this in our own churches and fellowships—in requests for sermons and classes and explorations dealing with "something more." More than what? More than what Enlightenment Humanism and Victorian optimism and scientific so-called certitude have been able to provide. And we as ministers, often ill-equipped by tradition, training, experience, and assumption, we are being called upon to respond to these inchoate requests for "something more." Spirituality is a public as well as private desire, a collective as well as an individual need. But let us be clear. Let us not rejoice too soon in this wave of spirituality. Let us remember that the longing does not per se create faith; the desire itself does not bring fulfillment; the hunger does not automatically lead to fullness. The longing, the

desire, and the hunger must be focused and answered with some form if they are to grow in the life of the spirit. Focused spirituality threatens our place in our familiar communities—families, workplace, neighborhood, and church, especially church. I think of the woman who came 300 miles to me for baptism; she did not wish, she said, to hurt the feelings of her local fellowship. I think of a colleague who wears a cross concealed from the congregation. I think of another colleague, recently returned from a retreat, who said to me, "Of course this retreat puts me at odds with some of my people. And I'm here to serve them. What do I do now?" We encounter resistance to growing in soul—in ourselves, and in others. We encounter it in subtle and not-so-subtle ridicule: in misrepresentation of what soul-life means, in outright opposition ("Look, if that's what you want, fine—but find another church."). I have come to understand the frequent opposition to Christianity among us as something more than bad memories of Baptist preachers, as more than legitimate anger with the Christian right, as more than reaction to Christian arrogance and cruelty. This opposition is also resistance to spiritual growth itself, and in some societies this opposition is institutionalized. Where then do I lead with all this prolegomena? To what I call the Great Surmise. Let me approach it this way.

Some things we do not surmise, but know. We know that we are finite, have an end. We know that behind every discovery and disclosure lies a mystery. We know that there is energy and order in this universe, the principle which Heraclitus (in 500 BC) named "logos." We also know that spirituality is not simply the product of fear, frustration, or bad digestion. We know that our yearning for meaning and fulfillment is given in our very being. So! Follow that yearning, need, reaching to its source, to our creation, to our

createdness and surmise with me, if you will, that this
yearning, this reaching, this need, is no accident, no
psychic atavism, but a reflection of that reality from
which we come. The Great Surmise says simply
this: At the heart of all creation lies a good intent, a
purposeful goodness, from which we come, by which
we live our fullest, to which we shall at last return.
And this is the supreme reality of our lives.

Note the metaphors. Even a Unitarian Christians like Scovel,
when he addresses the whole denomination, has to search for
synonyms for the word "God."

Mike Morran is minister of the First Unitarian Church of
Denver. In five of six sermons featured on his website, there is little
discussion of God and faith but when he preaches an Easter homily
that changes. To him the holiday confirms the idea that God is a
loving God, not a jealous God, and that the connection to the divine
is important. The soul does not care whether one believes in the
resurrection or not. Unitarianism rebels against the idea that Jesus
died for our sins, and one must believe in Him to be saved. That
makes Christianity solely a church of law. Instead Unitarians believe
in a church of love. The cry of Jesus on the cross: "[God] why have
you forsaken me?" is evidence that Jesus did not know what was
going to happen to him. With the message of love he preached,
however, he was content to accept his fate without having solved the
mystery of life and death. Easter says that nothing is finished. The
essence of humankind is always waiting to be reborn.

In Saint Louis Suzanne P. Meyers of First Unitarian Church
in Saint Louis bases her Easter sermon both on Luke and Bishop
Spong's book *Resurrection: Myth or Reality*. Spong is a retired bishop
of the Episcopal Church who debunks the myths of the Easter story
as contained in the New Testament much along the lines of Parker's
postulation. Having established that base, Meyers continues:

> When I read the Christian scriptures, it is clear that
> Paul and the writers of the four Gospels are like
> me, that is to say, they too are not sure, or at least
> they are not consistent in their thinking about what
> happened on that first Easter morning . The earliest

account we have of Easter is found in the letters of Paul. The earliest reference is in the letter to the church in Galatia, which biblical scholars place at approximately 50 A. D. or some 20 years after Jesus' death. Jesus and Paul never met. What Paul describes as his "revelation" of Jesus is not a physical body rather it is a vision of the resurrected Jesus. In Paul's recounting of the first Easter, there is no Joseph of Arimathea, no angelic messenger, no empty tomb, no women who visit the tomb and no resuscitated body.

In the Gospel of Mark, the oldest of the four Gospels, written 20 years after Paul, some 40 years after the death of Jesus, the post crucifixion physical appearance is not mention either. The idea of a bodily resurrection does not receive its first mention in the scriptures until some 60 years after the death of Jesus in the Gospel of Matthew, and it is present in only one episode. The idea of bodily resurrection becomes full and overt only in the later Gospels of Luke and John which were written from 60 to 90 years after Jesus' death... But that's just fine with me because I don't believe that the truth of Easter Sunday is found in stories of angels, or empty tombs or resurrection, or supernatural events. The truth of Easter is much more subtle than that...

What Theodore Parker was saying is this: what is permanent about Christianity is the religion of Jesus, the one he taught and lived even unto death. What is eternal is the ethic that he embodied. What is transient about Christianity are the miracle stories, and the myths... I don't know what happened on that first Easter morning, but that does not mean the Easter story lacks the power to move me, inspire me, and even transforms me.

Reverend Meyers has thus solved the dilemma of Unitarian Easter, much as has Kendyl Gibbons, by calling on the truths of

Parker's absolute religion.

Daniel O'Connell, Meyer's colleague at Eliot Chapel in Saint Louis, has a different way of stripping the transient from the Easter story. He is a rarity, growing up as a Unitarian in the 1960s. In his biography he states that he always felt comfortable in a Unitarian Universalist (UU) religious setting. As he put it: "It has been a place of refuge, a place of sanctioned exploration, a place of honesty without pat answers for me (although I may not have been able to articulate that when I was a child). I was active in LRY (Liberal Religious Youth), and served in a variety of capacities with UU Young Adults all over the country. Growing up UU as made me feel "different" but it has provided both spiritual freedom and a sense of responsibility to spread our good news." He calls his sermon *CSI: Jerusalem* after the CBS television series:

> These programs have popularized forensic science so much that more college kids are majoring in it. And jurors in trials have come to expect DNA, fingerprints, and irrefutable scientific evidence because that's what the TV shows promise. In one recent real life case, an 11-year-old girl pointed at the person on trial and said, "That's the man who shot my father." The jurors found him *not guilty*, and one explained, "I would have liked to see some evidence, like finding the gun with fingerprints."

> If the public has trouble with evidence that's only a few weeks old, what can we expect from two thousand year old evidence? The popular media may want us to focus on the grisly details of the death. That kind of news gets headlines, that kind of news can make people mesmerized like watching a traffic accident replayed on TV over & over & over again. The CSI version of the last days of Jesus would talk about loss of blood and hypobolemic shock. There would be attempts to fix blame, to insist that the importance was about death, not life.

In the Unitarian Universalist tradition, we reject the fixation on Jesus' death. We reject the "crime scene investigation." We say that the death of Jesus is not nearly as important as his life. Millions of people have been born and died. How do we approach the life and death of Jesus of Nazareth? In the book of Luke, at the crucifixion, Luke says that the women & the others who followed Jesus watched the scene, quote "from afar." Luke uses that phrase in several places. In the parable of the prodigal son. The father sees the son— "from afar." This is how we approach the meaning of the life and death of Jesus of Nazareth— from afar. Across centuries of time, oceans of foreign culture, and still! His life and deeds speak to us from beyond the empty tomb.

Jesus said to love God with all your mind and heart and strength. And to love your neighbor as yourself. These are radical, almost unbelievable things if you try to pick them apart, if you try to take them seriously. How are we to love God? By clothing the naked, healing the sick, feeding the hungry, housing the homeless, and comforting the afflicted. How are we to love our neighbor? Do we even know our neighbor? Is our neighbor next door?... Or is our neighbor a child in Sudan dying of starvation?

The life of Jesus meant a life of service to others, of the deep spiritual insight that the kingdom of heaven is at hand— the Kingdom of Heaven is available to us in this present moment, and it is also something to work to bring about for our children. The life of Jesus was about seeing past the small differences among people to embrace Love with a capital L. The life of Jesus— to me— was about moving to radical spiritual depth, the whole hearted embrace of social justice, and caring for those most in need.

He thus has fashioned a very modern Unitarian theological

baseline, translating the demands of the biblical Jesus and God to an action plan for life.

The comparison of modern Unitarian theology, per force, cannot exclude a major church because of unconventional beliefs, but the First Unitarian Universalist Church of San Francisco, so important to the growth of the denomination in the second half of the 19th century, seems to have a crisis of identity. On any given Sunday, there is a potpourri of guest ministers mixed with the ultra-liberal views of Senior Minister Greg Stewart. One finds every facet of Unitarian and secular thought, from Kendyl Gibbons' Humanism to interim minister John Robinson's theism. There are pacifists that deplore the use of atomic weapons on Hiroshima and Nagasaki, Buddhists that offer meditation, and intern ministers that discuss their childhood education. Strangely, San Francisco sermons frequently indict American institutions and conventional values, this in the church whose first minister, Thomas Starr King, lectured extensively across the West to keep California in the Union. In 2006, John Robinson was the interim minister at the church and spoke of what certainly must be classed as traditional Unitarian values. The sermon is titled *A Confession, I am a Christian Fundamentalist.* He rejected the common use of the word "fundamentalism" to explain:

> We have allowed the Jerry Falwells and Billy Grahams, and Pat Robertsons to claim, unchallenged, words that they have no special right to; we've handed them the copyright. We've let them hijack Jesus and "Christian" and "fundamentalist." I've decided: I am not going do it any more: not let them run away with a vocabulary to which they have no special right. I am going to fight for these words. They are not Christian Fundamentalists. If anyone is, it is we of this free religious tradition. "Fundamentalism" refers to fundamentals, the essence, the core, the essentials of the faith. It is those fundamentals that I want to get at this morning.
>
> It is common to associate fundamentalism with literalism, with taking the Bible as literally true,

word for word, as inerrant; to take it on blind faith. Unitarian Universalists are often afflicted with another equally harmful malady, the reverse one: namely "blind unbelief," of failing to see truth because we threw the whole thing out in Pavlovian knee jerk reaction. There are only two things that Jesus says are important. Remember, he said this as a Jew, as a keeper of Judaism. They are the fundamentals of Judaism and Christianity. These are two fundamentals:

The first is: "You shall love your God with all your heart, with all your soul, with all your strength, and with all your mind". That is the essence. That's all. But it is enough. It is simple to say – But is perhaps the most astoundingly difficult road for humans to walk. It is easier to focus on creeds, and legalisms, even Purposes and Principles. Anything more than this is additionalism. Most people who call themselves fundamentalist vary from those words; they are in truth Christian additionalists, not fundamentalists at all. Let's not get confused here. When Jesus said "God," he was not speaking about a bearded old man in the sky. He was not talking of a celestial peeping Tom. He did not mean a cosmic avenger. We in this free religious tradition are often so busy saying what isn't God, we forget to look at the divinity around us. Jesus meant something more than what we say God isn't. What he meant was akin to what John Cyrus, former minister in Milwaukee, meant when he talked of "God."

John Cyrus wrote that believing in God "is believing in life, all of it". God is the life of all; it is existence itself, and the power that brings all into existence. Believing in God means understanding that this world around us, is it, the whole thing. Loving God means throwing your whole self into life. It means daring your whole being in this creation, risking everything for living, for making love real. That is what Jesus did.

Robinson was followed in the ministry by Greg Stewart and Stewart's Easter sermon is incompatible with the long and distinguished history of the San Francisco church. It is a tirade against Christianity called *Easter for Skeptics*. Easter, to Stewart is the saga of the season that needs to be unpacked and debunked "as layers of lies that lay the foundation for false witness." It is the children in his story that recognize that Easter is "so innately false that they must call us for our foolishness." The attack on Christianity continues: "The bells ring - tell them it is the broken body of Christ that died for you take this and eat, says the unconvinced priest to the laity that leaves such stories unquestioned." He goes on to give his version of the Easter story as that of an unmarried blue collar couple to whom Jesus was born, who even though he was illegitimate by the standards of that day, did not let society label him as an outcast. Jesus took risks and positions that insured that he would become an outcast. Jesus used his brain and his brawn (?) to challenge the oppression of the underclass of his origins... thus he became a threat to the elites. Stewart then turns the Easter story to political rhetoric and shows that Jesus was no different from today's civil rights activists or war protesters. Stewart rejects the miracle stories of the Bible by admonishing his congregation not to confuse Easter with Halloween. To Stewart, one must live to the fullest today, because there is no guaranteed tomorrow. Thus he is a rebel in the denomination and undoubtedly not the only one. It certainly the right of any Unitarian church to accept or reject any religious or secular view, to indulge in political speech, or to indict or support today's society. That is guaranteed by the cornerstone of Unitarian non-creedal religion. Stewart demonstrates a very angry approach to religion that certainly can attract, among others, agnostics and atheists and persuade them to join, as the San Francisco church membership of over five hundred can attest. But Unitarianism also requires tolerance of all beliefs and this Easter sermon belies this.

A totally different approach to the Easter holiday can be found at the University Unitarian Church of Seattle. Minister Alicia Grace starts conventionally by describing the confusion and ambivalence that Unitarians feel about the spring holiday, especially when the church observes not only the traditional Christian Easter service with its hymns and Hallelujahs, but also the Jewish Seder and the Christian Unitarian Maundy service, a communion that represents peace. Grace maintains that the Unitarian celebration goes back to the denominations Christian roots and has every right to claim that heritage. The message, according to Grace, is that out of misery and sorrow can come something beautiful and the emphasis on the soul is always right. Unitarians must attempt to step out of the world around us with its wars and strife and let the soul open up to the sun of hope. Her homily is positive, heartwarming and recognizes the multi-faceted aspect of Easter, Passover and Spring Festival.

Christmas sermons also reveal a church and its minister's theology. David Herndon, minister of the First Unitarian Church of Pittsburgh, does this in a sermon titled *Jesus as a Liberal Leader*. He follows a path trodden by others, distinguishing the religion of Jesus from the religion about Jesus:

> As Unitarian Universalists, can we claim Jesus as a liberal religious leader? The question takes on special significance at this time of the year, when so much attention centers on the birth of Jesus. Even if we do claim Jesus as a liberal religious leader, do we believe that his birth warrants such grand celebration? Here a little bumper sticker theology may come in handy. Two people in this religious community, both of whom have considerable appreciation for the Christian tradition, have recently reported to me that they have seen a bumper sticker that says: "Never mind being born again. Just grow up."
>
> Whether or not we place great importance on the birth of Jesus, and whether or not we think that Jesus himself had the experience of being born again, we can admire the fact that he did indeed grow up, demonstrating remarkable spiritual maturity throughout his years of public religious leadership... On the one hand, the religion of Jesus understands

Jesus as a teacher, as a prophet, as someone who lived an exceptional life, perhaps even as someone in whose life we see especially clearly the radiant result of a deep commitment to love God and to love one's neighbor. On the other hand, the religion about Jesus understands Jesus as a savior, as a divine being whose death and resurrection makes possible the forgiveness of our misdeeds and shortcomings, as someone who rescues us by doing things we could not do for ourselves. It seems to me that if we want to understand Jesus as a religious leader, then we are better off with the religion of Jesus rather than the religion about Jesus, for a religious leader invites others to come along and join in the work, not just to sit back and let the leader do everything for them. Leaders may go first, but they do not go alone. Unitarian Universalists may be reluctant to embrace Jesus as a liberal religious leader because of our disagreement with some beliefs that have been common within the Christian tradition. One of these is the belief that what happens after death is more important that what happens in this world here and now. Another is the belief that Christianity is the only true religion.

Can Unitarian Universalists embrace Jesus as a liberal religious leader? In accord with our historic Arian, Socinian, Anti-Trinitarian, Unitarian theology, we can embrace Jesus as an ordinary human being, no more divine than any other human being, who lived an extraordinary life of prophetic religious leadership. We can find in his teachings a deep appreciation for social justice, expressed in his willingness to offer respect and compassion and acceptance toward everyone. And we can find in his life an inspiring example of spiritual maturity expressed as service toward others.

Herndon illustrates that Unitarians are able to fashion a message of faith based on Christian traditions without resorting to biblical miracles.

Marta Valentin, former minister of the First Unitarian Universalist Church of New Orleans, had the daunting task of celebrating Christmas in the space of the Jefferson Presbyterian Church after her church was severely damaged by hurricane Katrina and is now in the process of being gutted and rebuilt. Her 2005 Christmas sermon was titled *Paths to Love*. She relates the story of a Christmas trip with a Baptist minister friend when she was greeted by a stranger with the phrase "Jesus is the Reason for the Season." In her sermon, she marvels at the ability of professed Christians to accept the saying as a mantra along with the implied belief that the Christmas story is the literal truth. Valentin admits that the Christmas story does not make sense for many Unitarians, but she feels that the season does provide a light of hope and reason in a year of darkness, particularly true for a church as hard hit as First UU of New Orleans. Valentin also states in her sermon that Christmas brings love and hope and that is the reason for the season. Love and hope enable the belief in possibilities, and forgiveness, and with mercy and love in the heart, there can be peace on earth and a better, more joyful world.

The modern Unitarian church may not have a unified theology, yet, as it reaches back in history to Unitarianism's beginnings, common themes arise. Unitarianism is a religion free from dogma and accepts a broad spectrum of beliefs. Deists are able to share the pulpit with humanists, and while miracle stories have been rejected, the fundamental faith in the goodness of humanity, based on Judeo-Christian traditions, universally forms the basis for worship. Sometimes a minister will establish a historical context for the religious experience; sometimes it is based on modern events and challenges. This provides the wide range of beliefs that enables a person to make a rational choice. Where there is an appeal to the emotions there is success and growth; where there is a constant recital of philosophy or politics there is acceptance and often decline. The variety in Unitarian theology can be confusing and within one church can change dramatically with a new minister. But there is one constant: faith, while under siege, can be used to win the battle for the hearts and minds of congregants. In the end, that may well be the reason that Unitarianism has evolved and survived through more than four centuries.

EPILOGUE

This has been a journey through modern Unitarian sermons and lectures to reveal the full spectrum of the denomination's liberal theology. It is the remarkable quality of its non-creedal belief system that all of these can coexist in the same denomination. However, I want to challenge Unitarians to establish a new paradigm of faith and perhaps a new theology of hope. The question then arises of what this might be. Let us accept that each individual church has a religious orientation generally determined by its minister. There might be near unanimity in how congregations treat the major Christian holidays of Easter and Christmas. Often the Easter story centers first on the contradictions in the New Testament gospels and then on the personality and message of Jesus. At Christmas, probably to accommodate many Unitarian children who are in public schools, churches frequently act out the story of Jesus' birth as related in Luke, complete with biblical readings and Christmas carols. In both cases due deference is given to other religious holidays that fall in the same time period: Passover at Easter and Chanukah and Kwanza in December. Often there is reference to the pagan origins of the celebration and its symbols. This means that the holidays cannot be used for theological conclusions of any significance. But there is a nagging question there: Why is it that at these celebrations Unitarian churches are filled to capacity? Probably, it is because deep down, Unitarians, even those who are professed atheists, cannot escape their Judeo-Christian roots.

It was much easier to define a Unitarian theology in the 1840 time period than it is today. Then, graduates of Harvard Divinity School spread throughout the Eastern states and the Mississippi valley to preach Unitarian Christianity. Some were persuaded by Emerson and Parker to reject the miracle stories of the Bible, and their sermons reflected the rise of transcendentalism. The early Meadville graduates followed the same pattern. Channing and Parker dominated Unitarian thinking and thus its theology. It was Christian in nature, and the New Testament was read avidly for sermon topics and opening themes. Thereafter social issues dominated Unitarian preaching, the most prominent of which was slavery. The split of North versus South was very evident, but even southern Unitarian ministers generally could not defend slavery, and prominent ministers like Eliot in Saint Louis were mute on the point.

The striking characteristic of Unitarian preachers in the second half of the nineteenth century was their involvement in civic causes. They founded public schools, training centers for adults, agencies for the poor, day care centers for working mothers, sanitary commissions to heal the sick and major universities. They championed women's rights and fought corruption in local government. Many of their sermons were civic lessons with theology secondary. It was not until late in the century that the first humanist preachers emerged, with Curtis Reese in Des Moines and John Dietrich in Minneapolis. In the twentieth century, Unitarianism, with its strong orientation toward social action, spread across the country. Meadville connected to the University of Chicago, became dominant in training Unitarian ministers but resisted any attempts to impose a particular theology. Starr King Theology School in California joined in graduating young ministers and also left the choice of theology to its students as they sought congregational affiliation. In many of the major population centers Unitarian fellowships were founded and some grew into churches. Often a city might have a humanist congregation side-by-side with a theist Parkerite oriented church. In smaller communities, Universalist churches continued to exist, albeit with smaller congregations. When, in 1961, the American Unitarian Association merged with the Universalists to form the Unitarian Universalist Association, many congregations changed their names, but the landscape of the denomination as a minority in American life did not change. A few urban churches, however, did become powerful voices of liberal religion in their communities and in the nation, the most prominent of which were Washington under A. Powell Davis, New York City under Forrest Church, Tulsa under John Wolf and Marlin Levanhar, Saint Louis under Earl Holt, and Cincinnati under Ellsworth Smith.

Despite these diverse theologies, a constant thread runs through the writings of modern Unitarian ministers, be they in sermons or Berry Street lectures. With few exceptions, they exemplify their inability or unwillingness to talk directly about faith or to use the word *God*. Synonyms abound: The Holy One, The Infinite Power, The Mystery, and The Power of Creativity. Unitarians have faith in humankind, in each other, in society as a whole, in the future. But faith in a higher and spiritual sense, in religion or a religious experience, is undervalued and rarely brought to the fore even by Unitarian Christian ministers. Only one reason comes to mind that would explain this. Unitarians church goers have diverse belief systems, ministers are unwilling to offend anyone. Thus the power of the original Unitarian idea (and for that matter of Judaism) that God *is one* is too close to a creed and is therefore devalued. Faith is not so much under siege in the Unitarian church as it is something to be feared. And here it is time to return to Luther Adams' essay *A Faith for the Free*. He states:

> ... A faith worth having is faith worth discussing and testing. To believe that a fence of taboo should be built around some formulation is to believe that a person can become God (or his exclusive secretary) and speak for him... One thing that is dependable is the order of nature and of history which the sciences are able to describe with varying degree of precision. How long the order of nature will continue to support human life is beyond our ken. Probably our sun will one day cool off and freeze. Moreover everyone is condemned to what we call death. Whether beyond this death there is a new life is a matter of faith, of faith that trusts the universe as we have known

it...Whatever the destiny of the planet or of the individual life, a sustaining meaning is discernible and commanding in the here and now...One way of characterizing this meaning is to say that through it God is active or fulfilling himself in nature and history. To be sure the word 'God' is so heavily laden with unacceptable connotation that it is for many people scarcely useable without confusion...God (or that in which we have faith) is the inescapable, commanding reality that sustains and transforms all meaningful existence. It is inescapable, for none can live without somehow coming to terms with it. It is commanding, for it provides the structure or the process through which our existence is maintained and by which any meaningful achievement is realized...The free person's faith is therefore a faith in the giver of being and freedom. Human dignity derives from the fact that to be a person means to participate in this divinely given meaning and freedom of this reality. If we use the terms of historical Christianity, we may say that the man and the woman are made in the image of the creative reality. Under its auspices they become themselves creators.

It seems that even those who are well educated and relatively well off (in other words potential Unitarians) do want to believe in something but the denomination is not satisfying that need. Thus for the twenty-first century, Unitarians must fashion a religious experience that addresses this — perhaps even if it means changing their neatly compartmentalized theology. The tradition of being non-creedal must be preserved, but ministers must recognize that humans are religious beings, even those who will vociferously deny this. This means, above all, that the intellectualism in services must be augmented with open appeals to emotion.

Only one of the six principles of the Unitarian Universalist Association mentions a religious theme. All of them could well be used by any denomination and even by the Ethical Society. If one goes further and examines the stated sources of the belief system of the UUA, it is inclusive as far as moral and ethical thinking is concerned and does use the word *God*, but nowhere can one find the word *Unitarian* or *faith*. What is missing, then, is a reason to join the Unitarian church. Contrast this with the Identity Statement of the First Unitarian Church of Saint Louis: "We the members of the First Unitarian Church of St. Louis are a community of memory, hope, and reverence. We covenant with each other to be inclusive, religiously non-creedal, and dedicated to freedom of belief and conscience." This begs the question: Why do people go to church? Again the Saint Louis church tries to answer this: "We gather to offer a humanizing community for individuals of all ages which supports and encourages each person's life-long moral and spiritual growth, and the continued fearless examination of life's deep and important issues. We seek to educate the human conscience and live our faith daily to make the world a better place to live. Together we celebrate life's great moments and its important passages through worship and fellowship." This addresses not only the need of potential churchgoers to join a social community but also to celebrate religion.

Rah rahs and Hallelujahs have no place in Unitarian Sunday services. Book review sermons are also unable to stimulate faith. Ministers need to talk about religion, about deep feelings about life and death, and still express their emotions. Michael Tino, minister of the Unitarian Universalist Church of Mount Kisco, New York, addressed this topic in a recent speech given to the Central Midwest District Meeting of the UUA. He pointed out that Unitarian service formats must satisfy three senses: the visual, verbal and visceral. Too many services concentrate solely on the verbal. A congregation can be energized by emotions, exciting both young and old. Every segment of the service provides an opportunity to express faith and joy. It must address the problems people face and seek the comfort they need. Ministers must be inspiring, they must address the soul, and must appeal to a person's inner feelings. Even those who call themselves atheists or agnostics believe in something. Again, quoting Adams: "The only person who is really an atheist is one who denies that there is any reality that sustains meaning and goodness in the human venture. The true atheist is one who recognizes nothing as validly commanding. It is very difficult to find this sort of atheist, perhaps impossible."

Unitarians cannot strive to satisfy those who would insist only on reality but instead should focus on what it is that can and should be celebrated. Faith must no longer be under siege. It is the indomitable power of being alive that enables one to greet every day as a rebirth of the human spirit. It is faith in an unseen and unknowable power in the universe that makes for decency and morality in the world. It is a strong belief that evil, prejudice, pain, and darkness can be overcome by the fundamental goodness of mankind. Unitarians already come with a mandate to alleviate suffering, to educate, to accept all humanity without prejudice, and in true equality. They must establish a covenantal relationship between each other and their ministers and build a faith that can pass the test of time. They must reason together, celebrate together, perhaps pray together, and, above all, have faith together.

BIBLIOGRAPHY

Books:

Adams, James Luther, An Examined Faith, Boston: Beacon Press, 1991.

Ahlstrom, Sydney E, and Carey, Jonathan Sinclair, An American Reformation, A Documentary History of Unitarian Christianity, San Francisco, London, Bethesda: International Scholastic Publications, 1998.

Bebbington, David, Evangelicalism in Modern Britain, Grand Rapids, Michigan: Baker Book House, 1989.

Belsham, Thomas, American Unitarianism: Or a Brief History of the Unitarian Churches in America, Compiled from Documents Communicated by James Freeman D. D. and William Wells Esq. of Boston and from Other Unitarian Gentlemen in this Country, Boston: Printed by Nathaniel Willis, 1815.

Beverley, Thomas, A Compendious Assertion and Vindication of the Eternal Godhead of our Lord Jesus Christ and the Blessed Spirit, Paper addressed to the High Court of Parliament, London: Printed for William Marshall at the Bible in Newgate, 1694.

Bolam, Gordon C., Goring, Jeremy Short, Thomas, Roger, The

English Presbyterians from Elizabethan Puritanism to Modern Unitarianism, Boston: Beacon Press, 1968.

Briggs, John and Sellers, Ian, Victorian Nonconformity, London: Edward Arnold, 1971.

Bumbaugh, David E., Unitarian Universalism, A Narrative History, Chicago: Meadville Lombard Press, 2000.

Chodron, Thubten, Buddhism for Beginners, Snow Lion Publications, 2001.

Creswicke, Louis, Joseph Chamberlain, London: Caxton Publishing Co., 1904.

Dictionary of National Biography, Vol. XVIII.

Eaton, Clement, Freedom of Thought in the Old South, Durham, NC: Duke University Press, 1946.

Encyclopedia Britannica, 11th Edition, Cambridge: At the University Press, 1911.

Frothingham, Octavious Brooks, Theodore Parker, A Biography, Boston: James B. Osgood & Co., 1874.

Gleadle, Kathryn, The Early Feminists: Radical Unitarians and the Emergence of Women's Rights Movement 1831-51, New York: St. Martin's Press, 1935.

Gould, William H., ed., The Works of John Owen, Vol. XII, London: Johnstone and Hunter, 1850-1853.

Grodzins, Dean, American Heretic, Theodore Parker, A Biography, Chapel and London: The University of North Carolina Press, 2002.

Holt, Earl K., William Greenleaf Eliot, Conservative Radical, St.

Louis: First Unitarian Church, 1985.

Holt, Raymond V., The Unitarian Contributions to Social Progress in England, London: The Lindsey Press, 1952.

Horton, Walter Marshall, Theism and the Modern Mind, New York: Harper & Brothers, 1930.

Howe, Daniel Walker, The Unitarian Conscience, Harvard Philosophy 1803-1861, Cambridge: Harvard University Press, 1979.

Lamont, Calvin, Humanism as a Philosophy, New York: Philosophical Library, 1949.

Lyttle, Charles H., Freedom Moves West, Boston: Beacon Press, 2006.

Marsh, Peter T., Joseph Chamberlain, Entrepreneur in Politics, New Haven: Yale University Press, 1991.

Martineau, James, Essays, Reviews and Addresses, Vol. IV, Academical Religion, London: Longman Green & Co., 1891.

Mendelsohn, Jack, Being Liberal in an Illliberal Age, Boston: Skinner Books, 1995.

Parke, David, The Epic of Unitarianism, Boston: Starr King Press, 1957.

Priestley, Joseph, The Theological and Miscellaneous Works, Vol. IV, First Published in 1786, New York: A Kraus Reprint, 1972.

Rice, Madeleine Hook, The Life of William Ellery Channing, New York: Bookman Associates, 1961.

Robinson, David, ed., William Ellery Channing, Selected Writings, New York: Paulist Press, 1985.

Solly, Henry, Working Men: A Glance at some of their Wants, With Reasons and Suggestions for Helping Themselves, London: Bell and Daldy, 1863.

Tarrant, W.G., The Project Gutenberg EBook on Unitarianism.

Watts, Michael R., The Dissenters, Oxford: Clarendon Press, 1995

Webb, Robert K., The Unitarian Background in Truth, Liberty, Religion, Essays Celebrating Two Hundred Years of Manchester College, Barbara Smith, ed., Oxford: Manchester College, 1986.

Wilbur, Earl Morse, A History of Unitarianism in Transylvania, England and America, Cambridge: Harvard University Press, 1952.

Young, David, F.D. Maurice and Unitarianism, Oxford: The Clarendon Press, 1992.

Wright, Conrad, Three Prophets of Religious Liberalism, Channing, Emerson, Parker, Boston: Unitarian Universalist Association, 1986.

Publications and Manuscripts:

Annual Review, 1792, Priestley, Joseph, Three Letters dated 21 September 1791.

Buch, Neville, Preliminary Conclusions in the Search of Philosophical Grounds of Unitarian Identity, Meadville School of theology, Journal of LIBERAL Religion, Vol. 3, No. 2.

Edinburgh Review of Critical Journal, Eleventh Edition, Vol1, 1802

Fortnightly Review, Vol. 30, 1873, Chamberlain, Joseph, The Liberal Party and its Leaders

Webb, Robert K., Unpublished Manuscripts: Miracles in Unitarian

Thought; The Context and Consequences of Joseph Priestley Defining Unitarianism; Necessarianism.

Webb, Robert K., View of Unitarianism from Halley's Comet, in Transactions of the Unitarian Historical Society, Vol. XVIII, No. 4, 4 April 1886.

Webb, Robert K., A Christian Necessity, The Context and Consequences of Joseph Priestley, Paper given at the Seminar on Political Thought in the English Speaking Atlantic, 1760-1800, at the Folger Institute Center for the Study of British Political Thought, March 20, 1987.

Annual Review, 1792.

Hansard Parliamentary Papers

London Times, 20 July 1791.

Internet Material:

http://brittanica.com/ danielharper.org, Transcription of Hosea Ballou, A Treatise on Atonement.

http://religion-online.org, Tillich, Paul, The Eternal Now.

http://uua.org/aboutuua/principles

http://uua.org/uuhs/biographies

http://uuma.org/BerryStreet/essays:

1820, Channing, William Henry, How Far is Reason to be Used in Explaining Revelation.

1835, Ware, Henry Jr., The Best Means of Bringing our Lay Brothers to be More Useful in the Maintenance of our Religious Institutions.

1850a, Burnap, George W., The Importance of Systematic Theology and the Duty of Unitarian Clergy in Relation to it.

1853, May, Samuel Joseph, Reform as Affecting the Rights of Property.

1868, Everett, Charles Carol, The Faith of Science and the Science of Faith.

1897, Everett, Charles Carrol, Reason in Religion.

1919, Boynton, Richard W., Unitarianism and Social Change.

1958, Clark, Thaddeus, Unitarianism Reincarnate.

REFERENCES

1 Jack Mendelsohn, <u>Being Liberal in an Illiberal Age</u>, Boston: Skinner House Books, 1995, Pgs. 37- 45.

2 James Luther Adams, <u>An Examined Faith</u>, Boston: Beacon Press, 1991, Pg. 20.

3 Paul Tillich, <u>The Eternal Now</u>, <u>http://religion-online,org</u> , Chapter 7: Spiritual Presence.

4 Neville Buch, <u>Preliminary Conclusions in the Search of Philosophical Grounds for Unitarian Identity</u>, Meadville Lombard School of Theology: Journal of Liberal Religion, Volume 3, No. 2, Summer 2002.

5 Robert K Webb, unpublished manuscript, <u>The Emergence of Rational Dissent</u>, Pgs. 6-7.

6 David Parke, <u>The Epic of Unitarianism</u>, Boston: Starr King Press, 1957, Pgs.18-20.

7 Earl Morse Wilbur, <u>A History of Unitarianism in Transylvania, England and America</u>, Cambridge: Harvard University Press, 1952, Chapters II-IV.

8 <u>www.danielharper.org</u>, Article on Arminianism.

9 <u>www.danielharper.org</u>, Transcription of <u>A Treatise on Atonement by Hosea Ballou</u>, Fourth Edition, 1882.

10 David Bebbington, <u>Evangelicalism in Modern Britain</u>, Grand Rapids Michigan: Baker Book House, 1989, Pg. 167.

[11] James Martineau, <u>Essays, Reviews and Addresses</u>, Vol. IV, <u>Academical, Religious</u>, London: Longmans, Green and Co., 1891, Pg. 47.

[12] C. Gordon Bolam, Jeremy Goring, H. L. Short, Roger Thomas, <u>The English Presbyterians from Elizabethan Puritanism to Modern Unitarianism</u>, Boston: The Beacon Press, 1968, Pgs. 20 and 21.

[13] Ibid.

[14] Michael R. Watts, <u>The Dissenters</u>, Oxford: Clarendon Press, 1995, Vol. II, Pg 23, quoting Josiah Thompson's List of Dissenting Congregations, 1715 and 1773.

[15] W. G. Tarrant, The Project Gutenberg EBook of Unitarianism, London: 1912.

[16] Webb, Rational Dissent, Page 7.

[17] William H. Gould, ed., The Works of John Owen, Vol. XII, First published in London by Johnstone and Hunter, 1850-1853, Pg. 208.

[18] Bolam et al, 1968 Pg. 144, citing John Cummins, <u>The General Corruptions</u>, 1714.

[19] Nathanael Taylor, <u>A Discourse of the Nature and Necessity of Faith in Jesus Christ: With an Answer to the Pleas of our Modern UNITARIANS for the Sufficiency of Bare Morality or Meer Charity to Salvation</u>, London: Printed by R. R. for John Lawrence at the Angel, and Thomas Cockerill at the Three Legs, in the Poultry, 1700, Pgs. i and ii.

[20] Webb manuscript defining Unitarianism.

[21] Ibid, Section by Roger Thomas, titled <u>The Salter's Hall Watershed, 1719</u>.

[22] Robert K. Webb, <u>Miracles in Unitarian Thought</u>, Unpublished Manuscript.

[23] David Young. <u>F. D. Maurice and Unitarianism</u>, Oxford: The Clarendon Press 1992, Pg. 39.

[24] Webb, Miracles, Pg. 6.

[25] Young,1992, Pg. 28.

[26] Robert K. Webb, <u>A Christian Necessity, The Context and Consequences of Joseph Priestley</u>, Paper given at the Seminar on Political Thought in the English Speaking Atlantic, 1760-1800, at the Folger Institute Center for the Study of British Political Thought, March 20, 1987.

[27] Robert K. Webb, unpublished draft definition of Necessarianism.

[28] <u>The Edinburgh Review or Critical Journal</u>, Eleventh Edition, Vol.1, Oct. 1802 to Jan. 1803.

[29] Hansard, Second Series Vol.29.

[30] Hansard, Second Series, Vol. 29, Col. 1431-1464.

[31] London Times 20 July 1791.

[32] Three letters by Joseph Priestley, dated 21 September 1791, published in the <u>Annual Review 1792</u>, London: Printed by Samuel Otridge and Son, 1810.

[33] Robert K. Webb, <u>The Unitarian Background</u>, in <u>Truth, Liberty, Religion, Essays celebrating Two Hundred Years of Manchester College</u>, Barbara Smith, ed., Oxford: Manchester College, 1986.

[34] Young, 1992, Chapter 7.

[35] Young, 1992, Pg. 124.

[36] Dictionary of Unitarian and Universalist Biography, Unitarian Universalist Historical Society, Robert Asplund Biography by Alan Ruston.

[37] Ibid.

[38] Encyclopedia Britannica, 11th Edition, London: 1911, Pgs. 797-799.

[39] Dictionary, Martineau Biography by Frank Schulman.

[40] Frank Schulman, Unitarian Christianity prior to 1860, Paper given at the Prairie Conference, September 2000.

[41] James Martineau, <u>Essays, Reviews and Addresses</u>, Vol. IV, <u>Academical: Religious</u>, London: Longmans, Green and Co., 1891, Pg. 47.

[42] Ibid, Pg. 50.

[43] Op. cit., Webb, Pg. 142.

[44] Henry Solly, <u>Working Men: A Glance at some of their Wants: With Reasons and Suggestions for Helping Them To Help Themselves</u>, London: Bell and Daldy, 186 Fleet Street, 1863.

[45] Young, 1992, Pg. 156.

[46] Raymond V. Holt, <u>The Unitarian Contribution to Social Progress in England</u>, London: The Lindsey Press` 1952, Pg. 42.

[47] Ibid.

[48] Ibid., Pg. 44

[49] Ibid., Pg. 45

[50] Ibid.

[51] Watts, 1995, Pg. 328.

[52] Robert K. Webb, <u>The Unitarian Background</u>, in <u>Truth, Liberty, Religion, Essays celebrating Two Hundred Years of Manchester College</u>, Barbara Smith, ed., Oxford: Manchester College, 1986, Pg. 23.

[53] Ibid.

[54] Dictionary of National Biography, Vol. XVIII.

[55] Watts, 1995 Pgs. 353-354.

[56] David Bebbington, <u>Evangelicalism in Modern Britain, A History from the 1730s to the 1830s</u>, Grand Rapids: Baker Book House, 1869, Pg. 100.

[57] Young, 1992, Pg. 151.

[58] Joseph Priestley, <u>The Theological and Miscellaneous Works</u>, Vol. VI, <u>An History of the Early Opinions concerning Jesus Christ, compiled from Original Writers ; Proving that the Christian Church was at first Unitarian</u>, Book III, First published in 1786, New York: A Kraus Reprint, 1972.

[59] Young, 1992, Pgs. 24-26.

[60] Watts, 1995, Pg. 90.

[61] Ibid, Pg. 92.

[62] Young, 1992, Page 155.

[63] Kathryn Gleadle, <u>The Early Feminists: Radical Unitarians and the Emergence of Women's Rights Movement 1831-51</u>, New York: St Martin's Press, 1935, Pg.21.

[64] Ibid.

[65] Ibid, Pg. 38.

[66] Young, 1992, Pg. 30.

[67] Short, 1968, Pg. 236.

[68] Robert K. Webb, <u>View of Unitarianism from Halley's Comet</u>, in Transactions of the Unitarian Historical Society, Vol. XVIII, No. 4, April 1986.

[69] Young, 1992, Pg. 32.

[70] Ibid., Pg. 35.

[71] Ibid, Pg. 36.

[72] James Martineau, <u>Essays, Reviews and Addresses</u>, Vol. II, Ecclesiastical: Historical, London: Longman's Green & Co.,1891.

[73] Ibid., Pg. 479.

[74] Ibid., Pg. 473.

[75] Ibid, Pg. 144.

[76] Robert K. Webb, <u>Miracles in English Unitarian Thought</u>, Unpublished manuscript, Pg. 22.

[77] Wilbur, 1952, Pg. 370.

[78] Ibid, Pg. 379.

[79] Watts, 1995, Pgs. 604-605.

[80] Ibid, Pgs. 432-433.

[81] Wilbur, 1952, Chapter 18, passim.

[82] Ibid., Pg. 435.

[83] Louis Creswicke, <u>John Chamberlain</u>, Caxton Press, 1904.

[84] Peter T. Marsh, Joseph Chamberlain, Entrepreneur in Politics, New Haven: Yale University Press, 1991.

[85] Ibid.

[86] Joseph Chamberlain, <u>The Liberal Party and its Leaders</u>, Fortnightly Review, Vol. 20, 1873, Pg. 295.

[87] Fortnightly Review, Vol. II, 1865.

[88] Ibid., Pg. 166.

[89] Ibid., Part 2 in Vol. VII, 1867.

[90] David Bebbington quotes G. F. Nutall's <u>The Influence of Arminianism in England</u> as stating that Unitarianism was Arminianism of the head, while Methodism was Arminianism of the heart.

[91] Donald Davie, <u>Essays in Dissent, Church and Chapel, and the Unitarian Conspiracy</u>, Manchester: The Carcanet Press Ltd., 1995, Pg. 55.

[92] However in the second part of Davie's work, a series of lectures he gave at Notre Dame University, one finds an attempt at an apology. "I am afraid that my focusing on this span of years will aggravate the offense that I already gave in *A Gathered Church*, to Unitarians. I am sorry about this, and must ask Unitarian readers to recognize that my enquiry is strictly historical; and that uncovering what I cannot help but see as a successful duplicity in the early years of English Unitarianism is not meant to impugn the sincerity and high-mindedness of professing Unitarians at the present day." Yet a review of that 1976 work reveals that this new attack on Unitarians used many of the identical words almost twenty years later, but now coupled with an attack on Unitarian patriotism that would be worthy of a McCarthy.

[93] John Briggs and Ian Sellers, eds., <u>Victorian Nonconformity</u>, London: Edward Arnold, 1973, Pg. 33.

[94] Robert K. Webb, <u>The Gaskells as Unitarians</u>, in <u>Dickens and Other Victorians</u>, Joanne Shattock, ed., McMillan Press, 1988, Pg. 153.

[95] Briggs and Sellers, 1973, Pg. 1.

[96] Webb, 1988, Pg. 144.

[97] Ibid.

[98] H. S. Perris in the Inquirer 19 December 1903, quoted by R. K. Webb's undated manuscript <u>Miracles in English Unitarian Thought</u>.

[99] Wilbur, 1952, Pg. 384.

[100] Ibid., Pgs. 370-380.

[101] Conrad Wright, <u>The Beginnings of Unitarianism in America</u>, Boston: The Starr King Press, 1955, Pg. 10.

[102] George E. Ellis, <u>A Half Century of the Unitarian Controversy</u>, Boston: Crosby, Nichols and Company, 1857, Pg. XIX.

[103] Ibid., Pg. XX.

[104] Madeleine Hook Rice, <u>The Life of William Ellery Channing</u>, 1961: Bookman Associates, New York, Pg. 44.

[105] Ibid., Pg. 45.

[106] Ibid., Pgs. 80-81.

[107] Thomas Belsham, <u>American Unitarianism: Or a Brief History of the Unitarian Churches in America, Compiled from Documents communicated by James Freeman D. D. and William Wells Esq. Of Boston and from other Unitarian Gentlemen in this Country</u>, Boston: Printed by Nathaniel Willis, 1815. Quoted on Page 10, evidently by the printer in his Preface to the work.

[108] Sidney E. Ahlstrom with Jonathan Sinclair Carey, <u>An American Reformation, A Documentary History of Unitarian Christianity</u>, San Francisco, London, Bethesda: International Scholars Publications, 1998, William Ellery Channing, <u>A Letter to the Rev. William C. Thacher</u>, Pg. 78.

[109] Ibid., Pg. 97.

[110] Wright, 1986, Pgs. 60 and 61.

[111] David Robinson, ed., <u>William Ellery Channing, Selected Writings</u>, New York: Paulist Press, 1985, Pgs. 71-72.

[112] Ibid.

[113] Ibid.

[114] Ibid, Pg. 78.

[115] Ibid, Pg. 82.

[116] Henry D.D. Ware, Letters to Trinitarians and Calvinists, occasioned by Dr. Wood's letter to Unitarians, Cambridge: Hilliard and Metcalf, 1820.

[117] Daniel Walker Howe, The Unitarian Conscience, Harvard Moral Philosophy, 1805-1861, Cambridge: Harvard University Press, 1979, Chapter II passim.

[118] Charles H. Lyttle, Freedom Moves West, Providence RI: Beacon Press Blackstone Editions, 1952, Pg. 13.

[119] Ibid., Pg.24

[120] David E. Bumbaugh, Unitarian Universalism, A Narrative History, Chicago: Meadville Lombard Press, 2000, Pg. 113.

[121] Dictionary, Article by Evens.

[122] Clarke, James Freeman, The Five Points of Calvinism and the Five Points of the New Theology, found in http://www.uuchristian.org/historical-writings/james-freeman-clarke.

[123] Octavious Brooks Frothingham, Theodore Parker, A Biography, Boston: James R. Osgood and Company, 1874, Pgs. 150, 151.

[124] Emerson, Ralph Waldo, Uncollected Essays, The Dial, 1842.

[125] Dean Grodzins, American Heretic, Theodore Parker and Transcendentalism, Chapel Hill and London: The University of North Carolina Press, 2002, Pgs. 145 - 148.

[126] Frothingham 1874, Pgs. 229-230.

[127] http://www.uuma.org/BerryStreet/essays.htm, George W Burnap, The Importance of Systematic Theology and the Duty of the Unitarian Clergy in Relation to It, Berry Street Lecture 1850a.

[128] Bumbaugh, 2000, Pg. 118.

[129] Dictionary, Article by Dean Grodzins.

[130] Dictionary, Article by George McGonigle.

[131] Ibid.

[132] Dictionary, Article by Grodzins.

[133] Op. Cit., Berry Street Lecture, Samuel Joseph May, Reform as Affecting the Rights of Property, 1853.

[134] Clement Eaton, Freedom of Thought in the Old South, Durham NC: Duke University Press, 1940, Pgs. 300-302.

[135] Dictionary, Article by Dennis Landis.

[136] Ibid., Article by David Haberly.

[137] Op. Cit. Eaton.

[138] Material for the San Francisco church was abstracted from the History of the FUUSoSF in the sermon archives of the church, John Robinson and others, 18 October 2005.

[139] Dictionary, Thomas Starr King, Article by Celeste Deroche and Peter Hughes.

[140] Ibid.

[141] Op. Cit.., Berry Street Lectures, Everett, Charles Carroll, Reason in Religion, 1897.

[142] Curtis Reese, ed., Humanist Sermons, Chicago: The Open Court Publishing Company, as quoted by Horton, Walter Marshall, Theism and the Modern Mind, New York: Harper & Brothers, 1930, Pg. 54.

[143] Howard B. Radest, The Devil and Secular Humanism: The Children of the Enlightenment, New York: Praeger Publishers, 1990, Pg. 51.

[144] Lamont, Calvin, Humanism as a Philosophy, New York: Philosophical Library, 1949, Pgs. 69-71.

[145] William Greenleaf Eliot, Sermon Book 2, October 1907.

[146] Ibid.

[147] Op. Cit, Berry Street, 1919, Boynton, Richard W., Unitarianism and Social Change, .

[148] Charles H. Lyttle, Freedom Moves West, Boston: Blackstone Edition of the Beacon Press, 2006, Pgs. 31-33.

[149] Ibid.

[150] Abiel Abbot Livermore, Reason and Revelation, contained in Sydney L. Ahlstrom and Jonathan S. Carey, eds., An American Reformation, A Documentary History of Unitarian Christianity,

Middletown, Connecticut: Wesleyan University Press, 1985, Pg. 211.

[151] Moncure D. Conway, <u>Sermon and Discourse East and West,</u> May 1, 1859, Records of the First Unitarian Church of Cincinnati in the Cincinnati Historical Society Library.

[152] Dwight A. Mayo, <u>A Sermon Delivered on Assuming the Duties of Pastor at the Church of the Redeemer,</u> 1 February 1863, Records of the First Unitarian Church of Cincinnati in the Cincinnati Historical Society Library.

[153] <u>The Roman Catholic Church and Free Thought, A Controversy between Archbishop Purcell of Cincinnati and Thomas Vickers,</u> Cincinnati: The First Congregational Church, 1968, Pg. 7.

[154] Mayo, <u>Religion in the Common School, Three lectures deliversed in city of Cincinnati, in October 1869,</u> Cincinnati: Robert Clarke & Co., Printers, 1869. Manuscript in the Historical and Philosophical Society of Ohio Library.

[155] Charles W. Wendte, <u>What do Unitarians Believe, A Statement of Faith,</u> Cincinnati: Printed for the First Congregational Unitarian Church, 1877.

[156] George A. Thayer, <u>What Unitarians Believe?,</u> Cincinnati: The Embert & Richardson Co., 1906, contained in a book of sermons by George Augustus Thayer, Minister of the First Congregational Unitarian Church in Cincinnati.

[157] Ibid.

[158] Walter Herz, author of article contained in the Dictionary of Unitarian and Universalist Biography.

[159] Ibid.

[160] Eliot Papers, Series 2, 1833.

[161] Earl Holt, <u>William Greenleaf Eliot, Conservative Radical,</u> Saint Louis: First Unitarian Church of Saint Louis, 1985.

[162] Ibid., Introductory Essay by William A. Deiss, titled <u>William Greenleaf Eliot; The Formative Years (1811-1834),</u> Pgs. 12-13.

[163] Holt, 1985, Pg. 36.

[164] Ibid., Pgs. 36-38.

[165] Eliot Papers, Series 2, Fragment Notebook 1833.

[166] Ibid., Sermon, <u>The Son of God</u>, Pg.43.

[167] Eliot, <u>Discourses on the Doctrines of Christianity</u>, Boston: American Unitarian Association, 1868, Pg.7.

[168] Ibid., Pg. 29.

[169] Eliot Papers, Notebook 5, 1860, Pg. 108.

[170] Son of God, Pg. 27.

[171] William Hyde, Howard L. Conard eds., <u>Encyclopedia of the History of Saint Louis</u>, New York, Louisville, St. Louis: The Southern History Company, 1899, Pg. 2091.

[172] John William Day Sermon: <u>The Divineness of Jesus</u>, Church of the Messiah, April 7, 1907.

[173] Ibid., <u>If Men Believed in a Living God</u>, April 21, 1907.

[174] Ibid.

[175] Sullivan is an interesting case. He was a Catholic priest who became disenchanted with his religion and turned to Unitarianism. He was immediately accepted by the American Unitarian Society, feted and came to Saint Louis in 1926. He never could quite shake off his Catholic antecedents and in January 1927 preached a sermon titled *The Place of Obedience in Life and Religion.*

[176] Church of the Messiah, Articles of Agreement.

[177] Church of the Unity, Order of Service, December 1, 1912.

[178] It is also the only sermon found in Unitarian literature that uses a mathematical formula in a sermon.

[179] PRWeb release dated 13 February 2006.

[180] <u>Simple Gifts, The All Souls Journal</u>, September 2007.

[181] Thubten Chodron, <u>Buddhism for Beginners</u>, Ithaca: Snow Lion Publications, 2001, Pg. 54.

[182] From The Wisdom Of Buddha, Translated from the Introduction to the Jakata, New York: Citadel Press, Kensington Publishing Corp.,1968, Pgs. 6 and 7.

[183] Chodron, 2001, Pg. 54.

[184] Brittanica on Line, http://www.britannica.com/eb/ article-9126164/Wicca#214728.toc.

[185] Jennifer O'Quill, <u>Sources of Our Faith,</u> Chicago: Second Unitarian Church, Sept. 10, 2006.

[186] Burton D. Carley, <u>The Way Home</u>, Berry Street Essay, 2005.

INDEX

as historical figure, 126–28, 160–61
Puritans on, 29
teachings of, 165–66
in Universalism, xix, xx
Jews and Judaism, xxiii, 59, 71, 73, 109–10, 163, 165
Jones, John, 16
Judeo-Christian tradition, 169–71
justice, 89–90, 148, 166

K

Kendrick, John, 13
King, Thomas Starr, 55, 162
Kingdom of God, The (Maurice, F.D.), 14
King's Chapel, xiv, 30, 32, 37, 42, 47, 48, 74, 122, 154, 158
Kingsley, Charles, 15
Kroeger, Ernest, 98

L

Ladies Eliot Alliance, 98
language
crisis of, 141–42
regarding God, 134–35, 142–43
Lanzillota, Peter, 155
Last Supper, 66, 67
Lavanhar, Marlin, 131–32, 171
Learned, John Calvin, 103–4
Learned, Lucelia, x–xi, 105–6
Leavitt, Bradford, 56
Legate, Bartholomew, 5
Lester, Art, 134–35
liberalism, xxiii, xxv, 20–21, 123. *See also* liberal theology
Liberal Party, 22, 24
Liberals, Conservatives and the Church (Amberley), 24
liberal theology
influence on other denominations, 79–80
vs. orthodox theology, 32, 33–36, 45–47, 66
vs. transcendentalism, 55

Lieber, Arthur, 102
life after death. *See* immortality
Lindsey, Theophilus, 7, 8–9, 20, 34
Little, Robert, 53
Livermore, Abiel, 67–68
Liverpool, 13, 18
logic. *See* reason
London University, 12
Lord's Supper, 66, 67
Louisville, 41–42, 49–50
Lyttle, Charles, 38, 40, 136
Lytton, Bulwer, 19

M

Macondray, Frederick William, 55
magic, vs. mystery, 138
Malick, John, 80
Manchester, 15, 18
Manchester College, 12, 13, 20
Mann, Horace, 66
Marsh, Peter, 23–24
Martineau, Harriet, 25
Martineau, James
on deism, xxi–xxii
Encyclopedia Britannica on, 13
influences on, 15
liberal theology of, xv–xvi, 12–14, 21–22
Priestley, split with, 12, 17–18, 20–21, 27–28
on science, xxii
Massachusetts, 37
Mather, Cotton, 29
Maundy service, 165
Maurice, Frederick Dennison, 11, 12, 14, 17, 27
Maurice, Michael, 11, 17
May, Joseph, 32
May, Samuel Joseph, 32, 37, 52–54
Mayhew, Jonathan, 31–32
Mayo, Amory Dwight, 69–70, 72–73
McGonigle, Gregory, 50–51
Meadville Lombard School of Theology, 48, 124, 170

meaning, search for, 83–84

Mediator-Catalyst, The (DeWolfe), 116

meditation, prayer as, 83

Meland, Bernard, 142

Menace of Socialism, The (Dodson), 108–9

Mendelsohn, Jack, xiii

Methodists, 4

Metropolitan Museum of Art, 41

Meyer, Suzanne, 122, 141, 158–60

Mill, John Stuart, 19, 62

mills, industrial, 15, 18

ministers. *See also* sermon topics
   and challenge of diversity, 141, 171
   and congregations, 85, 111, 149, 152–53, 156–57, 173–74
   faith, reticence on, 171
   and intellectualization of religion, 134–35
   and non-creedal tradition, ix–x, 8
   women as, 123

Minneapolis, 58

miracles, 8, 99, 100, 159, 164, 167, 170. *See also* faith; orthodox theology

missionary activities, 16, 38–40

Mission Free School, 94

mission statements. *See* articles and principles

Mississippi Presbytery, 54

Mobile, 56

Monthly Repository, 12, 18, 19–20

morality, 13–14, 17, 20–21, 76, 89, 119

Morehouse, John, 147–49

Morran, Mike, 158

Morse, Jebediah, 33–34

Mother God (Church), 149–50

music, 98, 102, 106

mystery, vs. magic, 138

N

Nashville, 56

National League of Unitarian Laymen, 78

Natural Theology (Paley), 37

nature and natural laws. *See* science

"Necessarianism", 9

"Necessity of Cultivating the Imagination as a Regulator of the Devotional Feelings, The" (Martineau), 13

Neile (Archbishop), 5

New England Anti-Slavery Society, 52

New Orleans churches, 54, 167

New York churches, x, 41, 136, 144, 149, 171

Nicene Creed, xvi, 7

Nigeria, 133

non-Christian traditions, tolerance of, xxiii, 59, 120, 139–41

non-creedal tradition, ix–x, 8, 22, 25, 36, 75, 86, 167–68. *See also* liberal theology

Non-Subscribing Presbyterian Church, 134

Norwich, 25

O

O'Brien, Robert, 81, 84–88

O'Connell, Daniel, 160–62

O'Connor, Faergus, 19

O'Quill, Jennifer, 143–44

organists, 98

organized labor. *See* worker's rights

Origen, xix

original sin, xx, 7, 8, 20, 32, 53

Origin of Species, The (Darwin), 37

orthodox theology. *See also* Unitarian Christianity
   vs. liberal theology, 32, 33–36, 45–47, 66
   proponents of, 33, 67, 93

Our Heritage and Hope (Holt), 119

Owen, Robert, 19

Owenite movement, 19

Oxford University, 12

P

rehabilitation, 128–29

"Relation of Jesus to his Age and the Ages, The" (Parker), 45

religion. *See also* church, as an institution
abandonment of, xv
experience of, vs. creed, 147
freedom of, 113–14
intellectualization of, 113, 134–35, 173
need for, 173
outside United States, 59
purposes of, 83–84, 87–88, 120–21
in schools, 71–73

Religion, the Church and Our Mission in the World (Wolf), 129–30

Religious Convictions of an American Citizen, The (Taft), 78–80

religious imagination, 141–42

resurrection. *See* Easter

Resurrection: Myth or Reality (Spong), 158

revelation
Bible as, 35, 69–70
creation as, 145
in Protestantism, xxii, 14
vs. reason, 36–37, 96, 136
statements regarding, xxiv, xxv, 77, 120

Rhodes, Christopher, 91

Rice, Madeleine, 33

Right to Believe, The (Clark), 111–13

riots, 10–11

Robinson, Alson, 80

Robinson, John, 162–64

Rochester churches, 41, 49

Roman Catholics. *See* Catholics and Catholicism

Roscoe Club, 18

Rose Catholic Church, 71–73

Russell, John, 23, 24, 26

Russell, Lucy Channing, 41

Ruston, Alan, 12

S

sacraments, 8

sacred books, 74, 76, 82. *See also* Bible, The

Saint John's German Protestant Church, 66, 71

Saint Louis
churches in, 65–66, 90–122, 171
cultural aspects, 90, 93–94

Salem witch trials, 29

Salter's Hall meetings, 7, 25

salvation
in other denominations, ix, xix, 6
rejection of, xiii
in Universalism, xix, 30, 42, 56, 96–97, 114–15, 130, 151

San Francisco churches, 55–56, 162–64

sanitation organizations, 41, 55, 57, 94

schools, 71–73, 93–94, 123. *See also* education

Schulman, Frank, 13

Schweitzer, Albert, 126–28

science
compatible with faith, 14, 50, 60–62, 99–100, 106–7
contradictory to faith, 21
religious interpretation of, xxii, 75, 85

Scottish Presbyterian Church, 2–3

Scovel, Carl, 156–58

Search for Meaning, The (E. Smith), 83–84

secularism, 72

Seder, 165

segregation, 63. *See also* slavery

self-determination, 14. *See also* individual experience

Sellers, Ian, 26

sentimentalized moralism, xxi

separation of church and state, 21, 72–73

sermon topics. *See also* ministers
Christmas, 165–67
Easter, 111–13, 153–65
generally, xiv, 131–32